Hugh Smith, Alexander Jamieson

An Apology For, Or Vindication of the Oppressed Persecuted Ministers and Professors

of the Presbyterian reformed religion in the Church of Scotland: emitted in the defence of them, and the cause for which they suffer

Hugh Smith, Alexander Jamieson

An Apology For, Or Vindication of the Oppressed Persecuted Ministers and Professors
of the Presbyterian reformed religion in the Church of Scotland: emitted in the defence of them, and the cause for which they suffer

ISBN/EAN: 9783337298326

Printed in Europe, USA, Canada, Australia, Japan

Cover: Foto ©Lupo / pixelio.de

More available books at **www.hansebooks.com**

AN
APOLOGY
FOR, OR
VINDICATION

OF THE

Oppressed persecuted Ministers & Professors of the Presbyterian Reformed Religion, in the Church of *Scotland*; emitted in the defence of them, and the cause for which they suffer: & that for the information of ignorant, the satisfaction and establishment of the doubtful, the conviction (if possible) of the malicious, the warning of our Rulers, the strengthening & comforting of the said sufferers under their present pressurs & trials.

Being their Testimony to the Covenanted work of Reformation in this Church, and against the present prevailing corruptions and course of defection therefrom.

P R O V. XXIII: Verſ. 23.
Buy the truth & sell it not ; also wisdom, instruction, & understanding.

I. P E T. III. Verſ. 15.
But sanctify the Lord God in your hearts ; & be ready alwayes to give an answer to every man, that asketh you, a reason of the hope, that is in you, with meeknes & fear.

J U D. Verſ. 3.
It was needful for me, to write unto you, & to exhort you, that ye should earnestly contend for the faith, which was once delivered unto the saints.

Prestat sero, quàm nunquam sapere.

Printed in the Year 1677.

To the most Noble and Honourable
LORDS,
The Lords temporal of his Majesties Secret Council, in the Kingdom of *Scotland*.

Most noble and honourable Lords.

CAsting our eyes about us to see, under the wings of whose patrociny & protection, we should shelter the ensuing *Apology* or *vindication*; we could not, in our apprehensions, fix upon any so fited for this, as your *Lo.* who, by the station, & office you bear under his *Maj.* in this Kingdom, are constitute the protectors of the poor, the Releevers of the oppressed, & the breakers of every unjust yoke: the serious thoughts of which does afford us this confidence, that as our unjust oppressions make us objects, fitted for your *Lo.* compassion and justice; so your *Lo.* office, and what it binds unto, in the behalf of the oppressed, before God and men, will, on the ingenuous & plaine production of our reasons, for the justice of our cause, at length prevail, for breaking of these yokes of oppression now on us; and removing of their real causes. We therefore cannot but in charity and reason expect, that much humanity & justice, from your *Lo.* that was granted by heathen Rulers, to Ministers & Christians, in the primitive times of the Christian Church; of which we have in Scripture & History memorable instances. Was not *Paul Act.* 26:1. permitted by King *Agrippa* to speak for himself, who, in vindication of his righteous cause, deduced the grounds thereof, and cleared them so to the conviction of his hearers, that they judged him neither worthy of death, nor of bonds? Did not some of the Roman Emperours, upon the reading of the Apologies of the Christians, as of *Justin Martyr, Apollinaris, Mileto, Origen, Tertullian,* and others, declare their innocency, and mitigat the rage of persecution, that then prevailed against them? May not we we then, who profeſſe the ſame Proteſtant Religion with your *Lo.* entertaine ourſelves with the hope of the ſame favour & juſtice, that was ſhewed by Rulers, to the Lords people before us?

As our adverſaries calumnies & bitter reproaches, with which they labour to render us odious to all, eſpecially, to your *Lo.* are unjuſt and malitious; (being partly their evil and uncharitable deductions from our principles and actions, and partly groſſe & notorious lies; ſuch as the heathens charged on the primitive Chriſtians, who finding no juſt mater for their accuſations from their Profeſſion and behaviour, gave it out to the world, that they worſhiped the Sun, an aſſes head, and uſed promiſcuous copulation at their aſſemblies;) So it is the Teſtimony of our conſciences, that as a brazen wal does ſheild & uphold our Spirits from ſinking, under thoſe burdens, with which they have aimed to keep us at under with your *Lo.* We know, there is no new or ſtrange thing happened unto us, but what hath been the common lot of eminent saints, yea of Christ Jesus, our blessed Lord and Master; the servant is not greater then the Master; if they dealt so with him, no mervail they deal so with us. So great is the Testimony & witness of our consciences, as to all the greivous things, they have and do charge upon us, that we have hitherto possessed our souls in patience, and not opened our just and true greivances (as we might and should have done) for fear of offending your *Lo.* But perceiving the truth of the Gospel, the righteousness of our cause, and the welfair of immortal souls, are like to suffer thorow our too long silence, we have adventured to disclose our thoughts, and to give, so far as we can, a satisfieing account of the grounds of that faith and hope, for which we suffer. The God of Gods knowes, & Israel shall know, we use this fredom and plainness of speech towards your *Lo.* and all others, not from any contentious and ill affected ed humour; but from the sense of the obligations laying on us, for the conservation of the true interest of Religion, and the hope of relief for these from your *Lo.* which we most humbly beg and exspect, for the sake of truth and righteousness, that are now fallen in the streets, and fled into Corners. If on an impartial examination of what we have said, in the defence of our cause, and of ourselves for its sake, against the reproachs of our enemies, it shall be found that it is not just, but iniquous, we ask no benefite from your *Lo.* clemency and justice; let all severity be used. But if the cause of our former and present sufferings be righteous (in the confidence of which, we have been bold to give to your *Lo.* and the Christian world this sober ensueing account) we humbly entreat that protection and relief in its defence, which your power and station in this Kingdome do enable and oblige your *Lo.* to.

 Wherefore casting ourselves at your *Lo.* feet. We doe, in the behalfe of

* 4   pure

pure Religion &undefiled &the souls of all concerned therein, beseech your *Lo. Fi.ss.* That our just & well grounded exceptions against *Prelacy* & *Erastianisme*, may be taken into consideration & laid to heart: for if they hold good, will not the future consequences of these evils, to this land, your *Lo.* families, & posterity, be dreadful, who thereby are laid pen to the judgments, denunced in the the Word of God, against perjury and Covenant breaking? We doe not lay the stresse of our cause on the Covenants & Oaths, taken by this nation, against the foresaid evils or corruptions, as the primary and chief Argument (as will appear to all on the perusal of our subsequent *Apology*;) but on their opposition to the Word of the holy and true God: for, we grant, Covenants and Oathes, that are obligatory and binde to an observance, suppone their matter to be antecedently just, and do bring their primary obligation from it; hence the things contained in, & engaged to by Covenants and Oaths,
must

must be proven and made out to be necessare & righteous from the Word of God, before their obligation can be admitted & received; which we have laboured to doe, in this following discourse. And if from it, our Covenants and Oaths doe appear to be just, are we not assured, that the corruptions and sins engaged against by such divine tyes, and relapsed into contrare to these engadgments, doe provoke our Holy and righteous God, to the inflicting of all those plagues and judgments, threatened in the word against the violators of such sacred bonds? And if this be a truth; (as we hope none will deny) what can we then expect to our selves & posterity, if reformation & repentance doe not prevent, but ruine and desolation, according to every ones accession to these evils; which, no doubt, are crying for vengeance on this declining Church? *Next,* We pray your *Lo.* to consider, that we build our conclusions on no other foundation, then our worthy reformers in this

Church

Church and others, laid downe in their arguments and debates againſt *popery*; which for its want of, and oppoſition to the holy Scriptures, they have condemned for an Antichriſtian defection from the doctrines of Chriſt. We hold to the ſufficiency and perfection of the holy Scriptures, reſolving, thorow the Grace of God, to admit of no other rule of faith and obedience, in the maters of our God, but theſe: what they condemne, we muſt renunce; & whatſoever doctrins or practiſes, in the houſe of our God, want their authority and approbation, we cannot, yea dar not admit? The experience of the Church in preceding ages shews, what miſcheifs, the opening of this door, hath brought in upon her, to the almoſt uter ruine of all her concerns.

The preſent grouth of *popery*, and the quick advance it makes among all degrees of Profeſſors, in this and our nighbouring Churches, ſayes to all, &, we ſuppoſe, to your *Lo.* that the ſafety & preſervation of the proteſtant reformed

formed Religion, does, in all prudence, require, that its real and sincere friends should be encouraged, and not thus persecuted with violence; which no doubt, tends so to the weakening of the Protestant interest & cause, that in one of *Queen Elizabeths Parliaments*, it was as judged a sufficient reason, not only to restraine the rigide pressing of conformity, but likewise to encourage all Non-conformists, who, in those times, were looked upon as stout antagonists to popery, and such as might be employed, entrusted and made use of in opposition to it. Is it not to be feared, that the *Pope*, having his instruments and emissaries amongst us, for working out of his designes on these Churches, which, all his former engines have not hitherto effected; and finding, through our confusions and distempers, the occasion fitted for his purpose, hath no question, a secret active hand, in influencing and increasing of this violence; which, if the Lord, in his mercy to this many wayes afflicted and ruined Church, doe not prevent; will facilitat his longed for, & much endeavoured designes against the reformed Religion in these Ilands. And however we are represented to your *Lo.* as unfriends to Religion, and the interests of State (as if they must ruine if we stand) yet the experience of past and present times, beside our publick confessions, doth sufficiently witnesse, how malitious our adversaries are in this unjust calumny? We are no innovators, nor pleaders for innovation in Church or State; but do hold, adhere to, and resolve, through the grace of God, to maintaine the reformed Protestant Religion, against all sorts of enemies, as it is contained in the holy Scriptures, summed up, and breifly comprehended in the Confessions of faith of the reformed Churchs; especially in the Confession of faith, Larger & shorter Catachismes of this Church, in opposition to all *Popish*, *Arminian*, *Socinian*, and *Sectarian* errors and innovations. We hold for our maine & rooted

le, the holy Scriptures to
rd of God, the absolute per-
nly rule of faith and maners;
g any supplement of Ecclesi-
dition; yet we do not deny
its due respect, use & reve-
l although we maintaine, that
istian, of what rank & degree
ught to study, & be conver-
Scriptures; yet we acknow-
necessity and great use of a
anding Ministry, and re-
directive authority of the
not with an implicit faith,
the judgment of discretion.
the teaching of the Spirit ne-
o the saving knowledge of
ut absolutly deny, that the
ngeth new revelations in ma-
ctrines, worship & Govern-
t only that he opens the eyes,
htens the understanding, that
erceive and rightly take up,
f old revealed in the word by
Spirit. We rejoice in Christ
ving no confidence in the flesh,
or

or in a legal righteousnes; desireing to be found in him, who of God, is made unto us wisdom, righteousnes, sanctification and redemption; yet we constantly affirme, good works of piety towards God, of equity and charity towards men, to be necessare, both *necessitate precepti & medii*: our Ministers presse on themselves & hearers, the necessity of Regeneration, as the solid fundation of good works; & the severe, strict exercise not of a popish out side formal, but of a spiritual, real mortification and self denial. We extol all ordinances of divine appointment; but reject all humane inventions, especially religious and significant not institute ceremonies in the worship of God.

It ought to have no little weight with your Lo. that by using of such violence, the most sober, judicious, universally religious and industrious part of the subjects, and consequently the most useful and stedfast to his Maj. true interest and honour, are exposed to dayly vexation and trouble, to the great dammage

mage and prejudice of this Nation and Kingdom. We suppose that, upon an impartial view, it will be found, that the choice and better part of the subjects is dissatisfied with the Government, now introduced into this Church, and consequently obnoxious to the severity of the lawes, enacted against non-conformists: and of what dangerous consequence this may prove to Church and State, we leave to your *Lo.* most serious consideration. We know, the certaine issue of all maters, is known to God only; but if we shall take our measures, in conjecturing at future events, from the working of present causes, there is all rational ground to fear, that there are dismal and heavy times coming on this nation; which, by taking and fallowing of right wayes, in the present juncture of affaires, your *Lo.* may prevent; and if not done, will, no doubt, afford mater of bitter sorrow, & repentance to your *Lo.* or children afterwards. It is & shall be our hearty prayer to God, that your *Lo.* may have the Spirit

rit of wisdome, and of the fear of the Lord, poured out upon you, to foresee the evils, that are hastening towards us; and in time to hide yourselves, this Church & Kingdom from them.

Is it not apparent to all, that conscience does not act, nor lead our antagonists? Do not their opinions about Prelacy; their Profession of all readiness to comply with the contrare, if on foot; their frequent changes into the interests and formes of all preceeding times, how contrare soever to their once professed and sworn principles (while true Presbyterians remained constant and immoveable, thorow the times that went over their heads;) their covetous and licentious lives, discover their want of conscience in the courses, they now so furiously run? Let not your *L*. think, that it is his *Maj.* interests, (as they pretend) or any true consciencious regaird to these, that moves them to such obseqiuous compliance with the present lawes? Let the outward interests of this world be separated

rated from their way; and it shall soon appear, how void they are of true zeal for his Maj. and his lawes, as is evident beyond all denial, from their carriage & behaviour, in past & present times. As we have no external benefite to expect to engage us against conformity to the present lawes about Church Government; so we are to look, from our principles, and practises conforme thereto, no lesse then the ruine of our selves & families in this world: if conscience of duety towards God & this Church, according to the word, did not determine and move us, of all men we were the most foolish and miserable; but seeing our hearts, in the consideration of the justice of our cause, & of the sincerity of our intentions, in acting conforme to it, does not condemne us; we have this confidence towards God, that as we are acquit & shall be justified before him; so shall we be recompenced and rewarded. to the aboundant compensation of all outward loses; even for these things, for which we are condem-

** ned

ned of men; so that that which is esteemed our folly, sin and misery, is and shall be reputed our righteousness, wisdom and glory.

Albeit we have not the external advantages of power, riches and wordly policy, but the contrare to contend with, and endure; yet, seing the Word of God in our hands, doeth prosper and prevail to the gaining of immortal souls, the restraining of impiety, and the propagating of the savour of the true knowledge of Christ Jesus, in all places where it comes, notwithstanding of the opposition made unto us in this work; it will, on many accounts, be your *Lo.* wisdome, not to stand in contradictory tearmes thereto, least your *Lo.* be found to fight against God in the persons of his servants and people; for, we are assured, that this work and cause is of God, partly for its conformity to his holy word; & partly for its undeniable fruit and successe, in converting & saving of souls from sin, preserving and maintaining of its self, against the opposition it meets with on all hands; which we take for a signe of its being of God, as the Christians did of old in their debates for the Christian Religion against its adversaries, which under great opposition grew and prevailed exceedingly, although stript of all the outward advantages of worldly power and policy. If this cause be of God, and approven by him, as we nothing doubt,

doubt, it will not be in the power of the mightelt to crush it. Men may afflict and put us to great sufferings (which to them will be a signe of perdition, but to us of salvation;) but while this Church continues Proteſtant, and hath God abiding in her, their contradiction will be in vaine, as is hitherto manifeſt. And a thowſand to one, but it reſolve in their own ruine here & here after.

The mater of difference betwixt us and our adverſaries, being in their owne confeſſion (a popular argument they much uſe with the people) not foundamental, but indifferent, we humbly beg of your *Lo,* that for preventing of further confuſions in this Church, & attaining of the true peace of the ſame, you will be pleaſed, to conſider, whether it be better and ſafer for this Church, that the Chiſtian Reformed Religion be totally ruined among us, for ſatisfying of a few; or a thing indifferent, & far removed from the vitals of Religion, be taken away, and not thus enforced by violence on ſo conſiderable a part of the ſubjects, who, for conſcience ſake, cannot receive, nor ſubject thereto? And knowing that a ſerious and impartial examination of this one queſtion, if diligently purſued, would quickly determine your *Lo,* to courſes quite oppoſite to theſe now proſecuted with ſo much heat againſt us; we intreat your *Lo.* not to give eare to theſe calumnies

lumnies and undue representations of the present case of affaires in this Church, made by our enemies, the *Prelates*, by which they labour to instigat to all this unjust and unseasonable violence, that will Produce bitter and lamentable effects to this & the succeeding generation, if not prevented in time.

Most noble & honourable Lords, we cannot but take notice of that too common prejudice entertained against Presbyterian Government, & instilled with so much artifice by our opposits in the mind of many, on which, they have alas too much advantage, through the love of sin, & natural enmity at the wholsome severity and power of the Christian Religion, that is predominant in all unregenerat persons; to wit, the strictnes & impartiality of Presbyterian Government in its exercise, against all sorts of scandals, in all degrees of Professours, the great as well as the meane; for we know, that while Presbytery was up and in vigour amongst us, the zeal and faithfulness of Ministers, in reprehending all sorts of sins, and exercising of discipline impartially, conforme to the commands and ruls of the word, without exception of persons, is that which hath caused all this dislike of, and rigour against Presbytery; and conciliat that much respect to, and love for Prelacy, as to eject the one, & bring in the other. We will not now enter on the debait, whether this strictnes against

against sin be the native product of Presbyterian Government, when exercised conforme to its principles; or the contrare the genuine consequence of Prelacy, that necessarly results from its constituent & preserving causes? Which were no great labour to make out. But leaving this, we humblie entreat your *Lo.* to have that patience towards us, as to suffer us to say.

1. In conformity to the principle of the Christian profession, it must be, in the confession of all Christians, mater of sad regrait & lamentation, that in places, where the Christian Religion is owned, zealous faithfulness against soul destroying sins, should be admitted & received, as a prejudice against Ministers & their Government; which should commend & cry it up; yea that does endear it to all conscientious Christians, that rightly understand their owne Profession. Must it not be a terrible length, this generation is gone, in declineing from the power of Religion; when that, which is its excellency & glory in the sight of God & good men, is become the occasion & mater of its dislike & reproach? Can there be a fuller evidence and discovery of the predomining & prevailing power of naturs enmity, in Professours, over the life of true godliness; and their being given up to the lusts & sinful inclinations of their owne hearts, that thus sets them in opposition to the meanes, appointed for their delivery from the

** 3 domi-

dominion & power of damning sins: whither are we gone, and what may we expect will be the hight of our defection, and the judgment of it, if Professours put themselves in such a plaine & open professed contradiction to their Christian Profession? 2. Let not your Lo. think, we say this with an intention to justify any failing, in this mater, committed by any of our perswasion, that shall be made appear to be such from the Word of God, & our Professed principles. And although we cannot condemne all the instances, that are now disapproved by our antagonists; yet we grant, there were considerable escapes, in preaching & exercise of discipline, which were the effects of imprudence & passion in some, and of wordly inclinations & designes in others of corrupt minds; who to raise themselves in this world, and for that end, to gaine the favour of persons of leading influence & power, keept no measure, but rune to strang hights of zeal against some sins, while they connived at others; but seing by their compliances with the cryed-up cause of these times, they do now declare to all the world that they vvere never of us; how unjustly are their wicked follies imputed to our Government and vvay. But for all the instances given in against us, and the hideous cry raised after them, yet vve must say, the greatest and most common failing among Ministers, vvas in the defect,

defect, in that the most were not so diligent, faithful & impartial, in the application of the vvord to the sins of the times, personal rebukes & censures, as they should have been; as (alas) vvas too visible & observed by many; for vvhich novv they bear their rebuke, in that many of those are now become their cruel persecutors, to whom they were sinfully sparing & indulgent. Moreover, let it be granted, that many of these instances were in the excesse unjustifiable; yet if the constitution and principles of Presbyterian Government were not for, but against them, it cannot be charged with these: they must be the faults of the persons, and not of the Government; otherwise all Governments must be condemned, as guilty of all the mal-administrations, commited by Governours; which all acknowledg to be absurd? But when any of the contrare minded shall demonstrat these to be the native product of our principles for doctrine and Government, they shall be considered, & according to the conviction they give of the same, they shall be acknowledged. But will your *Lo.* be pleased, to consider the sad & deplorable extreme our antagonists are run into, who medle not with any sort of scandals, except a few and these in the meanner & lower degree of persons, over looking all in the more opulent and great; which hath encouraged wickedness to

lift

lift up its head, and to diffuse its self thorow all ranks without control, to the infecting of this Church with all kindes of scandals; which, no doubt, will resolve either into the total ruine of the Protestant Religion, or els in sad desolating judgments, on this land; and if it come this length (which we earnestly beg of the Lord he would prevent, by pouring out of a Spirit of repentance and reformation on us) where will be our advantage by *Prelacy*, that is now so much extolled?

Therefore not loving to trouble your *Lo.* any further, we shall adde but this humble and earnest request; that your *Lo.* would be pleased, to make some due and just representation of the true State and low condition of this Church, unto his *Maj.* who (we hope) through your *Lo.* intercession, will, in his wisdome and clemency finde out some just expedient, for relieving of this Church of her oppressing evils, under which she groans; and undoing of these heavy burdens, that lye on us: for which we are your *Lo.* humble petitioners, and had been so alittle sooner, if we had not been discouraged by lawes anent Church maters, that seems to us, to close all door of accesse to his *Maj.* and your *Lo.* for representing our just greivances this way. If we may not obtaine this reasonable and just request (as we suppose) there is not another refuge left us, but to referre our cause to the righteous tribunal of the just and almighty God, where your *Lo.* and we will stand on even ground, and have judgment passed without respect of persons. -

An

An Apology for, or vindication of the oppreſſed perſecuted Miniſters, and Profeſſors of the Presbyterian Reformed Religion, in the Church of *Scotland*, emitted in the defence of them, and the cauſe for which they ſuffer.

The Introduction.

IT is not unknown (as we ſuppoſe) to the Churches of Chriſt, in the Iſlands of Britanɛ and Ireland, and other parts of the Chriſtian World, what perſecutions, upon the introduction of Prelacy in the Year 1662. the partie, called Presbyterian, hath ſuffered, eſpecially in the Church of Scotland, and yet lyeth under, throw the implacable and violent rage of their adverſaries, the Prelates and their adherents: who having got the Civil powers on their ſide, have prevailed to the enacting of ſuch lawes, that theſe (who from the conſcience of duty towards God, and ſenſe of the obligations of their Covenants and Oaths, lying on them and theſe Churches, cannot comply with, nor give obedience unto) are not only expoſed to bitter and hard ſufferings, for a conſiderable time; but loaded with all ſort of reproach, and repreſented as rebellious and diſloyal to Authority, contrary to their known principles and actings. It is not the deſigne of this undertaking, to deſcend into the conſideration of the maine cauſe of our ſufferings, nor yet to lay any Odium on our Rulers, to the pre-

prejudice of their just authority; (as the righteous judge of the world knowes, and we hope will make manifest in due time) but to clear some Necessary truths and duties; and to vindicat some of our practises, from the unjust aspersions of adversaries; who by lies and unjust representations of our principles and carriage, do publikly and privatly defame and misrepresent to Authority and others, our behaviour under the present course of affairs: an artifice they have used of old and late, for ingratiating of themselves, and their interests, into the favour of our Rulers, and sharpening of the edge of persecution against us; in which they have had no small successe. If it were not for the Interests of truth and Religion, which, through the hot contests and debates of this times (actuated by ambition and covetousness, on the one hand, and the love of truth, on the other) are in hazard to suffer shipwrack, we incline rather to keep silence; and to possesse our souls in patience under the present violence, used against us; (as our too much silence hitherto does sufficiently witness) but finding that the interests of the Gospel, and the concerns of immortal souls, are struck at, and are like to suffer no small prejudice through our silence, we have put on a resolution, to give to the Christian world an account of the grounds of our practises, for which, we are this day, so much reproached and persecuted. And seing there is no accesse in the ordinarie road, to give a due and just information of our case, to our Superioures, by supplications, petitions and remonstrances, (allowed by scripture and natures light) by reason of the influence & power of our adversaries; we cannot but expect that much justice from all, as to excuse us, for doing of this, in this way, which the vindication of truth and of ourselvs for its sake, in the present juncture, make every way so necessary: for finding, in the present state of things, that we cannot, without betraying of the

Gospel

our immortal souls, (for which as Mini-
ians we are called to contend, on all highest
ny longer silence; but that we must give war-
he imminent dangers, that threaten Reli-
rity and power; we look upon it, as our
uty; by clearing truths and practises, (so
emned) to endeavour the prevention, and
from the snares, they are in danger of, and
wherefore, in all Christian sobriety and humi-
leave, to open our hearts and mindes to all,
erned in our case. 1. Anent the cruel and
lour used against us. 2. Our practise of
hearing of the Gospel of Christ, by Mini-
, yet adhering to the covenanted work of Re-
opposition to Prelacy and Erastianisme.
proving nor allowing of the late indulgence,
he preaching part of it, it hath been by some of
ctised. 4. and lastly, anent the Supremacy
as it is now established in his Majesties per-
d by law.

Sect. I.

Glasgow, with raisons why submission
ould not be given to Prelacy.

not to insist on the *first*, and if it were not
ed with some other things, that more
cause, and touch upon it, then any out-
of ours; we would incline rather to bury
ial oblivion, then thus to raike the ashes
esent actions; the mentioning of which
flect on some, whose reputation is dearer

to us, then they will readily admit themselves to beleeve: But we must not decline, what in the present case is necessarie for vindicating of our righteous cause, struck at and wounded through our sides. We shall only touch a few instances of many, that might be produced, and are yet fresh in the memories of this generation; and we fear (if Historians prove impartial) will speak to the disgrace of these times, in the succeeding ages. As *first*, That almost unparalleled Act of the Councel at *Glasgow Octob.* 1662. whereby at one stroke, a number of Ministers above 300, without all legal precedour, were violently cast out of their livelyhoods, and inhibited the exercise of their Ministery; and thereby a great number of Congregations laid desolate. And for any thing known to the Councel at their making and publishing of this Act, all the Ministers of the Church of *Scotland* (a very few excepted) might have been thrust out and ejected thereby, and so the whole Church laid waste, and dispossessed of the Gospel and it's ordinances; in which condition, shee might have continued long enough, to such a hight of prejudice and loss, which the much-cryed-up good of *Prelacy* could never have compensat, in this or the following age. Was it not evident (from the astonishment, that the disappointment of the designe of this Act had on our Rulers, in those that did not obey the law in subjecting to Prelacy, on it's emission) that it was passed without mature deliberation, and was influenced by the impatient Zeal & violent instigation of the Prelats, to the precipitation of all Counsels; which since hath been lamented, & not alittle regrated by many of that party, who have never, to this day, fallen on right methods & wayes of cureing

the

& confusions, caused by this act to the
amongst us. We remember of none like
of the *Interim* of *Germany*, in the time of
precedent, we think, that should not have
by any Christian protestant State, consider-
designe, & bad success to it's contrivers.
ing of this Act of Councel, it was not
l, that the Ministers ejected by it, were,
lity of them, young men, educated and
the Presbyterian principles; neither could
judgment, be supposed, that in such a
inexpected revolution of affairs, in
tate, persons of any conscience, could
moved to change the Principles they had
so long been in the practice of, without
of any convincing reason to the contrary.
inflict so heavy a punishment on Mini-
gregations, without any endeavours pre-
for their information, looks to be a
ond the bounds of charity and justice;
ding to all laws, Divine, ecclesiastick and
time and patience, in dealing with per-
the matters of God, for bringing them
ion of their errours, before the passing &
sentence; a piece of justice observed in
mes of Popery, and hottest persecutions
h of God, as is evident from the records
2. Besides, in all executions of laws
und transgressing the same, there useth to
entence, and infliction of the penalty, a
and conviction of the transgression; the
and priviledge of all subjects, observed in
rned States in the World, whether Chri-

stian

ſtian or heatheniſh: For, in the adminiſtration of juſtice to the ſubjects, there ought to be an application of the law to perſons, ſuppoſed guilty of it's violation, by a judicial ſentence, not only adjudging them to the penalty, but declareing the guilt, as the meritorious cauſe of ſuch puniſhments; which cannot be done, without a judicial trial and conviction, by confeſſion or witneſſes: But in our caſe no ſuch thing was obſerved, no not ſo much as an hearing allowed us.

Moreover, in this act, the Miniſters of the Goſpel were, under higheſt paines, diſcharged and forbidden the exerciſe of their Miniſtery, which they had received from the Lord, and not from the State; and this antecedent to any Church ſentence, or eccleſiaſtical conviction of guilt, deſerving ſo heavy a puniſhment: an encroachment on Church power, without a precedent in this Church, and in all others, except that of the *Interim* of *Germany*, condemned, on that very head, both by Popiſh and Proteſtant writters, as a reatch beyond the Limits, ſet to the Magiſtrats power, in the word of God, Is there not here a Puniſhment, formally eccleſiaſtick, inflicted by the Magiſtrat, without owning of the Church, to whom the infliction of ſuch puniſhments does properly belong; and by whom they were, time out of minde, exerciſed? But this with other Acts of the like nature, which followed, was ſuitable to the baſis and foundation, on which the new ſuperſtructure of Church government was founded and built, the Supremacy. How viſible is it from this act, the way uſed for bringing in of prelacy, the frame of the Acts of Parliament, anent it and the *Supremacy*, and the procedour in executing of the ſame; that

the

the designe was not only to subject the Church wholy only to the State, but to rob her of all power; which the prelates perceiving, laboured to help, in their after outting of Ministers not comprehended in this Act; some of them complaining, that Ministers should be exautorated by the Magistrat, without any Church sentence preceding: but more of this afterwards.

But supposing, this to be within the compasse of the Magistrats power; yet how unproportionat was the penalty to the alleaged crime? if there had been heresy in doctrine, or scandals in life & conversation, a justification might have been made of this sentence; but for simple non-conformity to prelacy, that had been by Church & State exploded from amongst us, as an high corruption in the government of the Church; and its reentry barred with the solemnest Covenants and oaths, that ever any Church or Nation came under: we say, for such a crime in such a case, to take from Ministers, as men, their livelyhoods; and as Ministers, their Ministery (dearer to them then their lives) is a punishment, when weighted in the ballances of equitie and justice, much beyond (we are sure) the demerit of the cause; especially considering, that the Persones imposeing conformity, and punishing others so severely for refusing it, were the same (for the most part) that had made and enacted lawes, severe enough against it. What? is prelacy a jewel of so much worth, that the Church of God cannot be well without it? have we not found the contrare, from the experience of past and present times? Although we should be judged uncharitable in this, yet we must say it, that they, who see not this, do either shut their eyes throw carnal interest, or wilfull prejudice,

against

against all evidence, that not only Scripture but the effects of Prelacy in this Church, affords to all men; Or els fight against their light. If we take our measures, by the true interests of the Church, or these things, wherein her true welfare does consist, we shall undoubtedly and undeniably see, that prelacy is not of that worth and use, to the Church of God, as to inflict such grievous punishments on Non-compliers with it: sure we are, soundness of doctrine, purity of worship and holiness of life have flourished in this Church, without it; and since its erection, these have come under a sad decay.

Obj. But many place the demerite of these severe punishments, in the disobedience to the lawes establishing Prelacy; the now great cry of these engadged in the present course, for justifying of all enormities, committed in the administrations of government?

Ans. To this we say, first, that all Divines and Lawyers assert, if non-obedience be seperated from contempt of authority, (as in many cases it may be) that the demerit of disobedience, is not rigourously to be pursued with punishments, especially of so high a nature, as these inflicted on us, for meer non-conformity; and the reason they give, is because, there are and may be such things in non-obedience, as will, to righteous judges, not only alleviat the guilt thereof, but discharge it from disobedience, let be contempt of authority; as invincible ignorance, inability, fits of passion, the tendencie of the thing commanded, in some cases, to the everting of the end of the law, which in such cases, is presumed not to be the will of the law-makers) the disposition & profession of persons to obedieinnce manifested, in all others things &c. if

our

our known and professed principles, extant in our publick confessions and treatises on this head, with our actions in all other matters relating to authority, be admitted and beleved, we will have as much to say, for freeing of our non-obedience to lawes, in this matter, from contempt of authority, as any. Give us the just liberty of our Religion, in preferring of God, our absolute and Supream Soveraigne, to all others; and in yeelding to him that obedience, he requires of us in his word, and none shall be found more obedient to Authority, in all things that do not intrinch on this. We do solemnly professe, and in the sight of the alseeing God, who searches the hearts and reins, that this, and this only, is the cause, why we cannot give obedience, to the lawes establishing prelacy, for upon all the search, we have made, we cannot find a warrant for it in the word of God, that perfect rule of Religion and Righteousness; but find it contrare unto & against the precepts and institutions of Christ Jesus, anent the government of his house. This being our perswasion, we are not able to evite the force of these obligations of our Covenants and Oaths, made to God and one another, against it; to the strick observation of which, we are by commands and threatnings contained in the word, most indispensibly bound, and from which tyes, no humane power can loose us. Is it not a sad matter in this case, that we meet with no other thing from any, for satisfying our consciences, and bringing us the length of cheerful obedience in this thing, but the cry law, law; which, in the matters of God, can be no sure bottome to our consciences; seing we as Christians are under a law, antecedent and superior to that of mens.

A5 *Secondly*

Secondly. Where the guilt of disobedience is truly found, yet the sentence passed against it, ought cheefly to respect the matter of the disobedience, and according to the quality and circumstances of it, the punishment should be proportionated: there are no divines or lawyers (that we know of) but hold this; and it is, beyond dispute, evident from the judicial lawes of the *Iews*, enacted and established by God himself, for the administration of justice, in that Commonwealth: for the guilt of disobedience being alike, in all deeds contrare to law, disobedience in smaller matters sould have as heavy punishments inflicted on the contraveeners, as in greater; which all acknowledge to be a strange solecisme in government, contrare to all natural equity and justice, the basis and ends of government.

Thirdly. And that our non-obedience to lawes erecting and establishing prelacy, is so high a crime in itself, as to deserve such punishments, as have been statute and execute upon us, we do not yet see; especially while we consider. (1.) The little evidence (as hath been said) for it in the word of God; Some of that party have racked their wits, for finding out its divine right and institution, as *Ioseph Hall*, and some others; but with so little successe, as hath forced many of them, to quite that plea, and take them to arguments of another nature. (2.) The confessions of some, who plead for the usfulness of prelacy, to the *well*, but not to the *being* of the political Ministerial Church; which they grant may be such without it, as most of the former opinion yeeld. (3.) Others that lean not to Scripture for the right of prelacy in the Church, found it upon Ecclesiastick constitutions, canons & customes; which they take

to

to be the Interpreters of Scripture in this debate, as *Dounhame* and others with him, that make most use of antiquity. (4.) Others more moderat, pious and more learned, then the rest, do so clip its wings, that they bring it to a meer constant presidency, in the meetings of presbyters, for government; making it a pure non-entity, as to what is established by law amongst us; and for which they bring no Scripture: of which judgment was that godly and learned Bishop *Usher*, who, for knowledge in all the controversies of the Church, especially in Antiquity, was *Nemini secundus*. (5.) Some others argue for it, as a matter of indifferency, that may be received or rejected, as Churches and States see it fits their interests; asserting, that all its authority and goodness depends upon and flowes from the power, that brings it in, thus *Stillingfleet*. (6.) Some of that party have fallen on a new method, for justifying its divine right (being straitened, as it seems, with our arguments, and the weakness of their owne) alleadging that Presbyters were not institute in Scripture times, by the Apostles; & that all Ministers, mentioned in the Scriptures, were Bishops, in the sense controverted, as Doctor *Hammond*; but his evidence from Scripture and antiquity, is so dimme, that (for any thing we know) he hath gained few, or none, to follow him in this. (7) These of the court party, place all its goodness in the authority & lawes establishing it; granting it signifies nothing antecedently to these. (8.) If we shall consider prelacy, and view it in its several parts, as it is by law constitute and setled amongst us, and bring them to the test and rule of the word of God, that we may give judgment of them, according to it; how little of prelacy will be found to be of divine right, even in the

the confession of our adversaries: of all that have appeared on the feild for its defence, there is none, that ever pleaded scriptural institutions, precepts and instances, for the Lordly titles, eminencies, and wordly dignities of the Prelats, that are now annexed to their office; nor yet for their civil places and power in the State; nor for their several orders, and degrees, as *Primats*, *Metropolitans*, *Archbishops*. &c: Or for the like among their dependents, in their numerous and various distinctions of degrees of superiorities, and subordinations; as *Vicars*, *Chancelors*, *Deans*, *Arch deacons*, *Subdeans*, *Deacons*, *Parsons* &c. whoever hitherto did put pen to paper, and contended for the divine right of prelacy, never opened a mouth to plead either Scripture or antiquity for these (except Doctor *Hammond* who argues for *Archbishops*: and what is prelacy, in its constitution amongst us, without them; The only thing debated betwixt us and our Antagonists anent it, is the superiority of one Pastor over other Pastors, and their respective congregations, to the probation of which, from scripture and pure Antiquity, there are two things, that must of necessity be made out from these: first the sole power of Ordination and Jurisdiction, and secondly Diocesan Churches made up of several lesser Churches and their respective Pastores and Officers: in these does the essential difference lye (in their owne confession) betwixt Bishops & Presbyters or ordinate Pastores; none of which two hath been proven from scripture and antiquity. And if that, which differences prelats from other Pastores of the Church, be not made to appear from scripture, how will their office be of divine right? and how can it be expected from us, who are under such strait, diving engadgments

against

hat we should comply therewith ; and
lawes, injoining conformity thereto. We
the subdolous and uningenuous way of our
this debate, who always keep in generals,
descend on the particular differences be-
es and Ordinare Pastores ; nor undertake
e : and the truth is they cannot : for they
confesse, that it is clear from antiquity,
rs have ordained, sometimes in conjun-
Bishops, and sometimes without them :
san Churches with one fixed pastor over-
Pastores and their flocks, we cannot meet
t probable evidence, from scripture and
: we find no argument from our adver-
ding this. It is empty arguing to say;
postles, there were Priests and Highpriests
stament ; there were seven Angels in the
es of *Asia* ; therefore there must be Bis-
If they will from scripture make out the
w assigned betwixt Prelats & Presbyters, in
s of the Apostles, Priests and Angels, we
cause. Let none therefore blame us, in
is as a necessare consequence of our Anta-
mbing in the probation of these things ;
among the Ministers of the Gospel, in
er or office, is of divine right ; for if
tion of the Ministery, there be alike po-
ll called thereto, there can be no superio-
ve another by divine right. (9.) It is
ich debated among the Popish school-
hich they are not agreed to this day; whe-
be an order or office distinct from that of
only a different degree of the same office
with

with Presbyters, including no power formally distinct from theirs: which last opinion asserts, that all power, acclaimed by the prelats, is formally in Presbyters; so that by office they are empowered to, and may doe all that the prelats pretend to. How hotly and stifly was this question tossed in the Councel of *Trent*, betwixt the *Italian*, *Gallican* and *Spanish* divines? which for this cause received no decision in this Councel, but was left undetermined as before; As is to be seen from the History of the said Councel. (10.) If any will consider our adversaries arguments for prelacy, and compare them with the arguments of Papists, especially *Bellarmins* for the Papacy, they shall finde, that they plead as strongly for the Pope or an Universal Bishop to the Catholick Church, as for the Prelat or Bishop, now controverted betwixt us, as wil be made appear by a particular condescension, if our intended brevity would suffer it. We referre such as question this to the arguments of both; and upon an impartial collation of the same, we nothing doubt, but it will be manifest. Doth not the much courted and endeavoured reconciliation with *Rome* by the prelatical party, in former and later times, with their concessions to them, for making way to this agreement, speak this with full evidence? As their denying the Pope to be the Antichrist; their granting a primacy to him over the Catholick Church; their purgeing the Romane Church of Idolatry and superstition; their asserting the difference betwixt Papists and us, in doctrine, worship and government, not to be fundamental, nor on their part damnable, &c. All which discover to the world the native tendency of prelacy, and what it will (if it continue) ultimatly resolve into. (11.) Do not

the

of prelatists, their practises, the ways
ɟing in and establishing of Prelacy among
on and condemne all the reformed Chur-
divines, (except *Scultetus*) who, in their
treatises & reformations conforme there-
:elacy, as no office of divine appointment?
dent to any that peruse them. We know
mphlet emitted in the beginning of prela-
duction, that undertakes to prove the con-
o destitute of all evidence of truth, that we
:dingly at the impudence & affrontedness
in alleadging of *Calvine, Beza, Bucer &c.*
who in their practise and writings have
bated against it. Did not this Author
their writings are extant, and others as
:herein as himself? But the unjust know
(2.) As prelacy or prelatical government,
ion and exercise, is a compound of addi-
Vord of God, which for want of its au-
ect; so presbytery or presbyterian govern-
:onfession of our Opposites, is, in all its
ie institution or right; which we offer to
i scripture and the concessions of our An-
ho first yeeld all our Church Officers
ɟg elders) to be of divine appointment,
nmond only excepted) granting, that
ordinare Pastores and Deacons, to be
he Apostles, and alwayes used in the
s day? they likewise grant the power of
jurisdiction in Presbyters, till of late;
:etings of Pastores lesser and greater for
nd discipline, and all the particularities
t these, asserted by and formerly exercised
among

among us? We think strange of *Stillingfleet*, in denying of Presbytery to be of Divine institution, who yeelds all we seek; for if all the former be of Scriptural institution and practise, must it not be of divine right, even as to its forme? We cannot forbear to declare our resentments to the world, of the high indignities done to our Royal and great *Master*, *Christ Jesus*, and his blessed word, the holy Scripture; in that. 1. The forme of the government of his house is asserted to be mutable, at the pleasure of men, and made capable of any forme they please to assigne to the same. Was it ever heard in the world, that the forme of any government was taken from the Officers thereof, and not from the Supream head, in whom the Legislative power is lodged? All that ever treated of governments, and spoke to their different forms, did always found their forms on the head, and not on the Officers of it? Is not *Christ Jesus* the *Supream* and *only Head of the Church*, by divine appointment? Are not ordinare Pastores or Presbyters found institute in the word, with all the parts of their power, that we afterwards grant to them? &c Will it not then necessarily follow, that the forme is of divine right, both in the head and officers; which is truely *Monarchicall*, and not alterable at the will of any? 2. For making way to this, the sufficiency and perfection of the holy Scripturs, as to matters of obedience and practice in the Church, is denied, and thereby the fundation of the Protestant Religion is shaken. How inconsistent is this with their granting the perfection of the Scripturs, in maters of faith? For if all maters of obedience be first and primarily Maters of faith, must not they be perfect in these also? How our

Opposits

(17.)

defend our arguments for the perfe-
ripturs, in matters of faith and manners,
ists (who in this speak more consequen-
Prelatists) and maintaine the former asser-
elligible to us. For our arguments plead
strongly for their perfection, in the one,
But must it not be a desperat cause that
op to support it? (13.) In the last place,
fer the following particulars to be consi-
nothing doubting that, when they are
usly weighted, it will soone appear that
is against Prelacy, are not light and
As 1. There is no good to the Church
souls attainable by Prelacy, that may not
hout it. It is a sure truth, that every
Divine institution hath it's proper good
1, in order to which, as it's end, it was
Christ, which is not easily reachable by
ces: As will appear to any on a particular
1: for as there is nothing defective in di-
ons; so there is nothing redundant and su-
ow we desire to know, what is that good
h and immortal souls, that cannot be ob-
ut Prelacy? let our Antagonists give in-
they think that ordination and jurisdiction
hat the Church hath by prelacy; we offer to
Scripture and antiquity (as hath been done
bout a reply, yea and granted by many of
Presbyters have the power of ordination
tion; and the truth is, it was never que-
y, but yeelded by all, till of late; for we
y instances in Scripture and antiquity, for
exercising ordination and jurisdiction; but

B   the

the reason, that all gave for it, was, that the ministery conferred by ordination, consisting of the power of order and jurisdiction, as it's integral constituent parts, persons ordained receive the power of both: If this be a truth, why may not the Church have these by Presbyters, as much to her advantage and benefite, as by Prelats? But some say, there can be no unity or peace in the Church without Prelacy. The contrare is evident from the Churches experience, in former & later times; for as the Church was never more rent, and filled with contentions and schisms, then under & by Prelates, of which there are innumerable instances in history; so there hath been much flourishing, unity and peace, under Presbyters, in Churches that wanted Prelats; as is to be seen in the present case of the reformed Churches, and will be evident to any that is acquainted with and seen in the records of the Church: what unity & peace hath the Churches of *Britan* and *Ireland* beyond other reformed Churches? Yea is there not more of these among them, then is with us, at this day? But what sayes unity and peace in the Church, if they have not truth and righteousness for their cement and foundation, which are seldome the attendents of Prelacy? But some place the good of Prelacy, in the oversight and inspection, it takes of Ministers and their respective flockes (of which they use to boast much;) But reason and experience do fully convince, and leave us beyond all Doubt, that this good, is as easily and better wine at, by Presbyters, in their associated and presbyterated meetings, lesser and greater, then by prelats: what can prelats do in this, that may not, and hath not been done by Presbyters, to the great benefite of the Church? as is manifest from the experience of

this

(19.)

this Church in preceeding times, and now not alittle confirmed by the contrare? Moreover in the act of restitution *Parl.* 1. *S.* 2. Act 1. it is given for one Reason, induceing to the bringing in and establishing of prelacy among us, that it is most suitable to Monarchy. What good this does or can bring to the Church, we cannot divine: we wish it had been instanced in the foresaid act: we know, the government of the Church, considered in its due latitude and extent, according to the presbyterian principles, is truely and properly Monarchical; for is not Christ Jesus the Supream and immediat head of the Church? and do not her officers act in her government in an immediat dependance upon and subordination to Him, as her King? So that if the Churches government being Monarchical be the good intended and meant, in this expression, it is as much attainable without prelacy, as by it; but we suppose, that this is not the good understood. *Next*, if by suteablenesse to Monarchy, be meant, that kinde of Authority and Dominion in Church-officers, in and over the Church, that is exercised by kings and Monarchs, and hath been assumed by prelats, since ever they appeared in the Church; this is expresly discharged and forbidden to Church officers in her government. *Matth.* 20, 25. *Luk.* 22, 25, How much Emperours, Princes Kings and States have smarted by this dominion, is known in history? Some say, it is the superiority and subordination of Church officers and judicatories, that is understood in this act; This may be had, and hath been attained in the Church, under presbyterian government, both as to officers and judicatories; the Pastour is superior both to Elders and Deacons &c. the classicall presbytery is

B 2

above

above the congregational eldership, & the provincial synod above the presbytery &c. *Obj.* there is not the superiority of one above the rest; *Ans.* but what good doth this either to Church or State? we know it hath brought much evil to both, but never any good, that might not have been wine at, yea and was not actually attained, without it; they that judge otherwise, are bound to give instances, which we earnestly beg they will doe: we know this brought forth the *Pope,* and did midwife *Antichrist* into the Christian world. But the thing, we suppose, that is truly intended, is the bringing of the Church into a slavish dependence upon, and subjection to the Magistrat; for which, we confesse, prelacy is every way fitted: how excellently did it serve the *Pope,* in establishing of his Dominion, and in bringing and keeping of all in subjection to him? and albeit since the reformation, the prelats changed their head, in taking on the Magistrat in the roome of the *Pope,* yet they retaine their use, which exceedingly endears them to worldly Princes, that affect domination in the house of God; but (as shall be proven afterwards) this is contrare to the fredome of Christs kingdome, his absolute supremacy and dominion over the same; and is inconsistent with Christain princes their professed subjection thereto; so that this is no good, but and evill destructive of the true concerns of the Church. 2. It is no small discovery to us of the evil and corruption of prelacy, that it is much approven, allowed and cryed up by all persones of profane, dissolute and debauched lives (except where it crosses their wordly interests) and the reason of this is obvious to all, for as corrupt and wicked nature does dislike all that is from God, as opposite to its wicked inclinations and wayes; so it
loves

loves, and is in much liking with all that is friendly to, and does encourage it in these. Is it not visible, that the encouragement, which flagitious and wicked persones find for their impieties, under the wings of prelacy, is the true reason and cause, for which it is so liked and cryed up by such? In this it is contrare to Presbytery in its due and faithfull exercise, which hath been, and yet to this day, is hated for its impartialitie, strickness and severitie against all sorts of scandal, in all ranks of persons high and low: for this we appeal to the general sense and observation of all in these landes: can we think that course to be of God, which for this reason is approven by the generality of the wicked? 3. Besides this, does not the prelates opposition to the godly (whom in rationall charity all are bound to judge such) in reproaching, oppressing & persecuting of them, to a strange hight of severity, who in profession differ only from them in a point, that depends on the meer will and pleasure of the Magistrat; we say, does not this declare, godlines to be their quarrel, and it to be inconsistent with, and contrare to their interests, which, we are sure, cannot be the effect of these means and wayes institute by God in his word, whose end and tendency is to promove godlines, and not to persecute and destroy it; as is now done. And whoever consider the constitution of prelacy, the rules for its exercise (to wit, the doctrines and opinions of prelats about Church-power and government) and the hight of Dominion, they lay clame to over the Church) will see, that of its self, it must be an enemy to true godlines, while it crys up its forme, and layes it self out for advanceing of it, in opposition to its power. 4. It is received for a sure truth, among all protestants, that as the renewed nature of the Godly does hate, and is an enemy, to all that is contrare to, and deftructive of true godlinefs; fo it is the evidence and figne of the evil and finfulnefs of a caufe, when it is disliked & oppofed by the generality of the truly fober, judicious and humble Godly. If we shall apply this to prelacy, as it is eftablished and exercifed amongſt us at this day, have we not caufe to fufpect its corruption, and to judge its defcent not to be of God? feing it is univerfally difliked and hated by the truely Godly; which eminently appears in perfons converted from wickednefs and fin, in which they lived before converfion; what ever likeing they had to prelacy, or hatred to presbytery, immediatly upon their converfion, they drink in an averfation from and hatred of prelacy, and love to the contrare. We know, this was *objected* by *Independents* againſt presbyterians, when the controverfy about Church government was hot betwixt them? But. 1. This objection was without any true caufe, as *Independents* were forced, afterwards, and at this day, to confeffe; they finding upon trial, that the Godly of the Presbyterian perfwafion, were exceedingly more numerous, then the other. 2. The difference betwixt them is very fmall (which may be incident to perfones truly Godly, and confiftent with their grouth and exercife of godlinefs); and if there were a healing condefcending temper, might be healed and removed; their difference lying mainly, in the authoritative fubordination of Church judicatoriesand con ftitution of Churches, as to the qualities and engadgments of their conftituent members; which when their one nefs in all other things about government, and their conceffions to one another, in the

little

little they differ about, is confidered, might be quickly accomodated and taken up. But it is other wayes with prelacy, in its conftitution and exercife with us; which, in its effects, attendants, and the bafis it is fetled upon, is found to be fuch a corruption in the government of the Church, and inlett to others in Doctrine and Worship, that it becomes truely hateful to all the Godly, that give themfelves up to the conduct and light of the Scripture, and make them their rule in the exercifes of religion and godlinefs: far be it from us to think or fay, that there is none of the prelatical gang, truely godly or pious. We know there hath been, and do beleeve, there are fome fuch among them; but O how few, and how much have thefe few been looked upon, and perfecuted by the reft, with an evil or jealous eye, fo as they have been judged more ours, then theirs? we have not forgot the diftinction, that on this head, was made in former times among the Bishops themfelves, and how they were diftinguished into *Puritan* and *Court Bishops*. Will not one of thefe two follow, either, that the generality of the Godly, (whom Chriftians walking according to the rule of the word muft efteeme to be fuch) are under a ftrong delufion in their opinions about, and oppofition to Prelacy; Or els (which is moft likely for the reafon formerly given) that Prelacy favours not of godlinefs, but in its native tendency is an enemy to it; which fayes it cannot be of God, but for trial and correction? 5. As the maine and chief qualification, the prelats require in their intrants into the miniftery, and in the people they admit to ordinances, is fubmiffion to, and owning of them conforme to the prefent law, how infufficient and

B 4   fcandascandalous soever they be, (which is overlooked and dispensed with in them); so their bitter opposition to and unceslant persecution of pious, able and faithful ministers, that comply not with prelacy, declares to all, that it is not the good of the Church (that consists in true knowledge and godlines) they seek; but the extending and establishing of their tyrannous dominion over all, by ministers and professors submiting thereto, without gainsaying of their impositions and commands. How contrare in this, is their way to the rules given in the word, for calling & ordaining of ministers, 1 *Tim.* 3: 1, 2, &c. *Tit.* 1: 5, 6, &c. and the practise of the Apostle *Paul, Phil.* 1: 15. who rejoyced Vers. 18. that Christ was preached, altho out of envy and opposition to him? Can that course be of God, which must be supported by such wayes and means, that crosse the directions and rules of the word anent Ministers, and disappoints the ends of the Gospel and Ministery? Beleeve this who will, we cannot.

Sect. II.

What moved Ministers to submit to the act of Glasgow: *& some remarks upon the* acts against conventicles, *and* such as refuse to depone against delinquents.

IT Hath been often *Objected* to us, both by friends and enemies; why did Ministers and Congregations obey so quickly that act of the Councel at *Glasgow*, in leaving and deserting of one another; seing, by vertue of their divine mutual relation to one another,

ther, as pastors and flocks, they were bound to cleave together, in performing and doing of all mutual duties, which by divine precepts and engadgments, they were bound to observe? *Ans.* As we will not altogether justify our cariage, in that and several other particulars, in our way thorow these sad times; (being willing to take with, and humble our souls for, all our imperfections and failings, that shall be discovered to us by any;) so there were some things, in the circumstantiat case, that may plead for us, and alleviat the offence taken at our too general practice in that matter; As. 1. The suddenness of that act, which allowed very little or no time for deliberation, and coming to any solide resolution, in a matter of such weight and unusuall practice, anent which, we had so few precedents in former times. All know, how puzling surprisals use to be; and if there be not a present divine hand to guide and support, under the power of temptation, with which surprisals are ordinarly attended, all are in hazard, thorow the byasse of corruption, to miscary, and in their resolutions to turne to the wrong side: Ministers and Professors are men of the same corruptions and passions with others; and whatever obligations be on them for truth and righteousness, and the leading of others, in the same; Yet throw darkness, the influence of corrupt affections, and temptations concurring therewith, (to which they are obnoxious as much, if not more, then others) they are ready to slip; in which, for the gospels sake, they should be pitied and prayed for.

2. It had no little influence upon us in determining our resolution to this, that our party, in our nighbouring Churches

Churches in *England* and *Ireland*, upon the emission of an act of Parliament, disenabling all Ministers, that did not conforme to Prelacy, for the exercise of their Ministry, had quit their charges, and removed themselves to other parts; not thinking it safe to themselves, their people, the interests of religion, as it then stood, to justle with Authority, in continuing their Ministery with and among the people, contrare to the new lawes made against them; while we considered this leading example, with the reasons moveing them to it, we thought ourselves as much pressed therewith, as they. And, no doubt, if we had followed the contrare course, our Loyalty had been sadly reproached, and their practise made use of to aggravat our disloyal disposition (with which we had been often branded, although falsly) to a great hight of contempt; which had, we grant, too much weight with us.

3. The maine designe, we had under consideration at that time, that did most exercise our thoughts, and take them up, was, how we might be preserved from the grand corruption, *Prelacy*, that did then enter into the Church: many questions, in order to it, were debated among us, for our mutual strengthening against the assaults of our common adversaries, which we, in rational fore sight, did apprehend would come upon us; never dreaming of this course, that was followed with us; which with one stroke cut the Gordian knots of many difficulties, with which we had often grapled, in our exercises and debats. In this unexpected course of providence, clearing our way, under many difficulties, we then thought it our happines, in being rid of, and delivered

vered from many a snare; which, no doubt, made us give place more easily to the penal part of that act.

4. We being at that time unacquainted with suffering, and contending for the truth, in opposition to prevailing corruptions, in this way, it is not to be expected in rational charity, that we could come so suddenly, to that hight of resolution and courage, as to venture on the utmost of hazards, that then did threaten the contraveeners of that act, and the laws upon which it was founded. *Suffering for righteousness Phil.* 1: v. *last*, is imported to be a gift, as far above the strength of nature, in our sinful imperfect state, as that of faith; as all finde when it comes to be their case. It is easy for onlookers to censure and condemne the failings of others, in persecuting times, but it is not so easy to suffer: it requires the Spirit of power, love, and of a sound minde, which is not quickly wine at by them, whom Christ calls to take up and bear his crosse. We grant this gives no discharge of guilt, in not doing and suffering, as God cals; yet it cryes for compassion and forbearance from others, who, on this consideration, should be spareing in their censurs, knowing they are in the body, and liable to the like snares and infirmities.

5. As that deed was too much influenced with fear, and other corrupt passions and affections, both in Ministers and People, (which did visibly predodomine at that time,) so there was a palpable desertion on the spirits of all, that rendered all counsells dark and perplexed, and in all deliberations, inclined to that which was freest from suffering, and positive compliance with *Prelacy*. Altho this doeth not
diminish

diminish sin, nor warrant any sinful neglect, nor give any true ground of excuse for it; yet it cals for charitable constructions from others, where sincerity is apparent in the maine; as then it was to the conviction of all; yea to the refuting of these hard, unchristian, and bitter censures of many, who judged our former professions of Zeal for the work of reformation, in preceeding times, to have flowed from a corrupt byasse to the world and the things of it, discovered, we grant, in too many, formerly seeming Zealots, by their compliances at that time; from whom they tooke their measures, in judging of others.

6. It is to be adverted, and ought to be of great weight, in the consideration of this busines, that Ministers, consulting their congregations, especially the godly and judicious among them, were advised to lye by for some time; and the truth is, they seemed as unwilling to venture on the hazards of suffering, that threatned all, as Ministers. This we know was the reason, that most determined not a few, to that resolution and practice: and what could Ministers do in this case, especially, in so sudden a revolution, anent which they had the leading example of others, in other parts of the Iland?

Notwithstanding of all these, and much more, that might be said for charitable constructions of Ministers and Congregationes practice in this, at that time; yet we judge it the infirmity and sin of Congregations and Ministers, that they did not cleave to one another as Pastores and flocks. We doe not plead for Ministers keeping to the accessories of the Ministery, as kirks, stipends, manses, glebs, &c.

which

which was, by divine precept, their right, but not in their power to hold; but we assert it was sin, that they continued not in the exercise of the Miniftery, paftoral over fight of the flocks, keeping up the government of the Church, we had been in the poffeffion of; and peoples not adhering to their Minifters, in hearing, and receiving of ordinances from them, and not affording them all due incouragement and maintenance; all which was done by Minifters and Churches, in times of forer perfecution then ours.

If the rigour and feverity, that by this act, and its full execution, with others that followed thereon, for a confiderable time, (which we forebear to mention) had ceafed, and gone no furder, we would have looked on all, as little, and laboured to have borne the fame, with that patience, meeknefs and refolution, that becomes Minifters & Chriftians, profeffing the name of Chrift Jefus: but the engines and devices, that afterwards were fet on foot, as the *High commiffion*, and feveral unchriftian & illegal practifes; with the over violent preffing of the people to a conformity in their capacity; with fuch illegal and inhumane ufages by military force, (which alone without any ftated and formed defigne, gave the rife to that infurrection, in the Year 1666. and the blood that followed thereon, to the the full conviction of our Rulers, who then fearched unto the bottom of that affaire) were ftraines fo high; that cannot be juftified by the moft extended rules of Chriftian moderation and equity, that Rulers are bound to follow, in the exercife of government: although this heat of violence, was for fome time,

a little

a little cooled with a shour of blood, and other dangerous consequences like to ensue; yet afterwards, fuel being by the *Prelats* brought and administrat unto it, it againe begins to take fire, and to break forth into strange kinde of laws, made (as it seems) to give a legal face to its proceedings; which in its former height it wanted; the the bounds of which it cannot yet keep, but (according to its genious) over the hedge it leaps, and gives a straine beyond these. It would be tedious to take an exact view of all the particular lawes made against us, by which, the foundation of our past and present sufferings have bin laid, and are like to be continued: therefore we shall only give instance in a few, from which, we may take our measurs, judging of the rest.

As, *first*, *Parl.* 2. *Carol.* 2. *Session* 2. *Act.* 5. intituled, *an act against conventicles*: As this act condemns all assemblies, convocations and meetings of the subjects, not expresly warranted of his majesty; (which will make many meetings and convocations of the subjects, now in use, illegal and unlawful) so by consequence, reflects on the meetings, and assemblies, that Christ Jesus while here, his Apostles, Ministers and Christians held, in the primitive times; who not only keeped their meetings without, but against the acts and edicts of the magistrat, in these times: for if it be laid downe for a foundation in government, that the only right of convocating the subjects is proper to the Magistrat, what ever be the causes, occasions and ends of them; then the Apostles, Ministers, and professours will be found transgressors and enemies to government; who, although inhibited and discharged from meeting, yet did not

for

forbear to assemble themselvs for worship and government. What a miserable strait are we brought to, that the meetings of the Lords people, now called *Conventicles*, cannot be condemned. but on the same grounds, the assemblies of the Church in persecuting times, must be judged dangerous, unlawful & seditious? But this is not the worst; for in this act not only preaching and expounding of scripture, by Ministers of Christ Iesus, (although in a family beside their own) is judged to make a conventicle and an unlawful meeting; but prayer also (a common duty of Christianity,) is declared to be of the same force; so that no nonconforming Minister or any other may pray together, on any occasion, or for any cause what so ever, but they shall be reputed keepers of conventicles, and liable to the penalties adjudged by this law to such. Is prelacy come to this height of opposition to godliness, that it cannot stand and be secured, except the worship of God in Christian societies be laide aside, and its exercise discouraged (to which there needs no such incitments in these times, the generality of professors being prone enough of themselvs to prove negligent and slack in this matter) under the odious names of *Conventicles*, and by such penalties against them? Are we such odious abominable creatures, that none must joyne in Christian communion with us, in these means and duties of worship, that are of common obligation on all Christians; but it must be forborne and laid aside? or if we once open a mouth to and for God, in any society; we shall bring ourselves and others under the hazard of so severe penalties, which, in the pursuance of this law, have been inflicted on some, to the astonishment of its hearers? But moreover all such meetings, beside the imputation of sedition and other horrid evils, with which they are branded, are represented, as the seminaries of separation and rebellion: a charge, if true, that maketh them meritoous of far heavier punishments, then some of these decreed against them: but from whence can this come? Not from the nature of these exercises, considered in themselves, which are nothing, but the performance of some necessary commanded duties of Religion, which all know to be the greatest means to, and cements of union and obedience, in Church and State: not from the mater that is preached and prayed; our principles for worship, doctrine, & government are known, being extant in our publict confessions, which are of a contrare tendency.

If any say, we preach principles of separation and rebellion. They, who assert this, are bound to make it out, of which we have heard nothing as yet, and should have been condescended on, and given for the ground of this act, and not the performance of these truly religious exercises, done by persones authorized and enabled thereto, by the commands of God. We require of all engadged against us, to do us that piece of common justice, they owe to all men, in the like case, that they will instance in the doctrines we preach, and in the mater we pray, wherein our meetings are become the seminaries of separation and rebellion, if they can: when this is done, we shall either give a satisfying answer to the charge, or els succumb to this act.

It is like, some place this charge, in our disobedience to the law. Then it comes from the law and the

the Law makers, and not from these meetings and the persons that keep them; for antecedent to this law they were not in themselves seminaries of separation and rebellion, according to this objection: and if this be the effect of the law, it had been more safe to have forborne it, whose work should be, rather to prevent and remove the seeds of rebellion, then thus to sowe them. But this law in its narrative suppons these meetings to be such, antecedent to its enacting; but gives no hint at any reason for this heavy charge.

Others again fix the truth of this charge on our meetings, for our withdrawing of the people, from the allowed publick worship, and the persons authorized by law to dispense the same. If the act had only circumstantiated and described such meetings, as had this effect, and not taken in all religious Christian fellowship in the duties of worship, something might have been said for justifying of this act, in a conformity to the principle of Church-government, now setled by law, without a wound to true piety; but to make all meetings of Christians, wherein any part of worship is exercised (without an expresse licence from the *prelat*) seminaries of separation and rebellion, is in effect to condemne Christ, his Apostles, Ministers and Christians, who, in opposition to Heathenisme, Heresy, Profainnesse and shisme, have, under severe laws made against them, assembled and met together, for communion in the worship of God; whose assemblies have been accounted unlawful Conventicles, and loaded with many of these evils, that are now charged on ours. Dar any, professing himself a Christian, say, that the meetings of Christ, his Apostles and Ministers, in houses and feilds, (who had the occasion of the Synagogues, the ordinare allowed places for meeting in worship) were guilty of separation and rebellion, (although charged with these) or did sow the seeds of these evils? Although none will affirme this, yet we undertake to make it out, from the frame of this act, as it now stands. Oh that such a law should be found in the records of this Nation, which will speak (if ever we returne to ourselves) to the shame and disgrace of these times. But, as to our separation from the authorized publict worship, with which, some with great confidence, brand us, we shall consider it afterwards, and see whether they or we be the separatists.

We forbear to speak to the penalties statute in this act, against the contraveeners of it; which on many accounts might be made to appear, to be far beyond the demerite of the crime, and an imitation of the popish cruelty, who punished the Professors of the truth; with punishments equal to those inflicted for treason; in which this act is not short, that adjudge the keepers of field Conventicles, to death and confiscation of goods.

In the next place, it adds not a little to our grief, under our present sufferings; that although there be penal lawes against *Papists*, and other heterodox persons, yet no notice is taken of them, nor any execution of the law upon them; yea in one act of Parl. *Caroli. 2. Session 2. Act. 7.* they are exeemed from the guilt and severity decreed against us: which seems strange to us, when theirs and our principles, even in matters of civil government, are compared; theirs,

in

ffions of all *Proteſtants*, are found to be
le with, and ſubverſive of that obedience
ice, that is due from ſubjects to magi-
oſed by them heretical: which was the
f the ſevere laws, made againſt them,
ie time, (from the beginning of the re-
were put to ſome execution; but as to
on now, ſlackened and and laid by, as an
t of date. Are their principles and deſigns
r their number any fewer? yea is it not
beyond what they have been ſince the re-
But poor we are laid open to the lash of
aws, enacted againſt us, and all wayes
ſh us and our cauſe, who owne no other
but theſe, that are either implicitly or
fferted, by all *Proteſtants*, which are
: world, to be corroborative of govern-
uch as make way for all juſt obedience
oject to the ſame.

way for the full and ſure execution of this
s another enacted Parl. *Caroli*. 2. *Seſſion*.
tituled *an act againſt thoſe, who refuſe to*
delinquents; which is particularly de-
omeing at full information, againſt Con-
Conventicle *keepers*; as is expreſſed in the
act; but ſo conceived and framed, as
that oath *de ſuper inquirendis*, uſed by
their inquiſition; (condemned by all
Divines, for its oppoſition to juſtice,
quity) for *firſt*, no ſort of perſons are
ie Father againſt the ſon, the husband
vife, &c. were the relations never ſo
ception of them is made in this act,

C 2   which

which use to be admitted in all other crimes, except that of treason. Next by this act, the deponent (whoever he be) is obliged to answer all interrogations and questions proposed to him, although he hath had no previous consideration of them, which in all other crimes used formerly to be allowed; that so the deponent might answer from mature and sure knowledge, which here is not granted. What a foundation is hereby laid for the molestation of the subject? Shall we be that unmerciful and unjust to all men, yea to our nearest and dearest relations, as to reveal that of them, which, if keept secret, brings no prejudice to Church or State: And if revealed, will ruine them, in this present world; and that for a mater, that antecedent to the law, is no transgression before God; but the doing of a necessare duty? An invention (we must say) framed against the good and consciencious, who cannot escape by this law; and for the encouraging of the bad to the persecuting of such, who throw the power of their lusts, are at liberty to say, and do, what they list. Are these the fruits of *Prelacy*, that most endeared it to us? Whither are we gone? Shall we thus fight against heaven, to reach a poor handful of persons, that are able to do nothing, but to look up to God, and sigh to him, for these evils, that, no doubt, are procureing and bringing dismal and sad dayes on this land? We forebear to anatomiz these and other acts of the like nature, and to give judgment to every clause and part of the same; but leave them to the impartial consideration of all concerned, to whom the effects thereof may afterwards speak more, then we love to utter, at this time. Only, in all humility,

lity, we offer two things, to be observed (which are the observations of not a few) that these and other acts do pave the way to all sort of cruel persecution, if a furder declension in religion shall happen to follow; (which we beg the Lord in his rich mercy to this nation would prevent.) Rulers are subject to erre, in the matters of God, as well as others; (as the instances of all ages leave beyond debat;) and if others shall arise after us, that incline to *popery*, or any other false Religion, are there not lawes made to their hands by us, that will facilitat their work, and make it most easy? What have they more to do, but to rescind some, very few in regaird of these that once were, and to execute those they finde in force and on record, for the persecuting of all opponents, to the height of crulty. Next there needs no act of Parliament to this change, and introduction of another Religion: an act from the King, recorded in the Councel bookes, and sufficiently published (which is declared to be of sufficient force and obligation about this mater) is enabled by law to do all. An act without a precedent in this nation, when considered in its full latitude and extent.

From what is said anent these acts, any may gather the true reasons of our refuseing the Bond (lately framed by the Councel) that takes us engaged against Conventicles, (as they are called) and was enforced by violence on us. Not pretending to much knowledge in the lawes, we have alwayes understood, bonds to be voluntare, and first to proceed from persons found guilty, and sentenced by the judge, conforme to the law; which the clemency of the Magistrat doeth often suspend or remit, upon the guiltys

C 3   offered

offered and voluntare engagment for better behaviour, in times comeing; and never required of nor imposed on persons, not proven nor found guilty. The truth is, if this violenting imposition of bonds, be thus allowed and practised, what ground will there be thereby laid down, for the trouble and molestation of the subjects? And who can promise to himself security from the oppression of others, that, out of malice or covetous designes, may, on any pretence, give information against others, altho never so quiet and peaceable?

SECT. III.

The Ministers preaching and peoples hearing vindicated: and foure Objections answered.

HAving thus far opened our hearts, and touched at some things, that are truly greivous to us; not so much for what we have suffered, as for the fear of what is like to be the consequences of the engines, framed and set on foot, for perpetuating ours and the Churches oppressions, in this and the following generations: we shall in the next place give an accompt of our practise, in preaching and hearing of the Gospel, dispensing and receiving of ordinances, at and from the hands of the ejected Ministers; the new cause of these heavy acts, sentences and punishments inflicted on us, for the same: in doing of which we shall, first, in all singlness of heart, bring forth the true grounds and reasons, binding our consciences, to these practises; and then shall take off the exceptions that are most used against us.

Our

se, in this mater, we build on such foun-
: all Christians, especially Protestants,
their professed subjection to Christ Je-
r King and Law-giver in the house of our
ound to own and adhere to, and from
annot recede, without contradicting of
ession, and doing manifest violence to
vord of Christ, the holy Scriptures, our
nd law-book, in all matters of doctrine,
d government. If on bringing out
, it shall be found, that our condemned
ese stands justified, we hope with much
e shall be acquited in the sight of God,
sciences of all that have any feeling and
Religion; the censures and talkings of
t us (which do not a little afflict us, for
equences thereof to themselves) shall
ve us.

: *first*, the Ministery of the Gospel be-
tive institution and appointment from
, as Head and King of his Church; and
qualified for, and called thereto, in his
without dependance on the Powers of the
; thereby constitute his Ambassadors and
and in special delegation sent from him
reach the Gospel, to treat with sinners
ation, and obedience; they by vertue of
on, and their special delegation or mission
are bound to exercise the Ministery &
are invested with, till it be taken from
way, by which he coveyed and confer-
e upon them. If this be a truth (as no
it doth acknowledge the divine authority

rity of the holy Scriptures, and subjecte themselves to its light and direction, will get refused) will it not follow that Ministers, in their ministerial capacity, are first and immediatly subject to Christ, and not to men, in their ministrations of the Gospel? for they as his Ambassadours, having and deriveing all their power from him, are obliged on highest paines, be reason of their special relation to him, and their comission from him, (which containes all their instructions) to do the work of the Ministery, & cannot be superseded therein by any, far less by them, that acknowledge Christs authority, in and over the Church, to be superior to, and above all other authorities whatsoever. If they had their power and mission from men, well might they submit to these, in taking it from them; but it not being so, they cannot think themselves discharged of their office, but in the way by which He conferred the same upon them. Beleeve us, in this lyeth a great part of our difficulty: we are sure, Ministers are Christs messengers, sent by him, whom they are bound to serve, in preaching of the Gospel and dispensing of ordinances, for the salvation of sinners, from which obligation none can loose them, but Christ Jesus, their only master and head in this work. (2.) It does also natively flow from the former truth, that all, especially those in and of the Church, are, by vertue of Christs supereminent, supream, and absolute authority, and their professed subjection to him, indispensibly bound to subject to the ministerial authority and its exercise, in the persons of those whom he sends, and that on the account of their ministerial power & office, which is truely Christs and not theirs; they

they acting according to the instructions contained in their commission: for they are Christs servants, serving him by special delegation in the Gospel, to which they are impowered, commissionated, and instructed by him; they bear his name, stand in his stead, and represent him to his people, as his Ambassadours, being sent by him to all sinners, for attaining and carrying on the great ends of the Gospel, their conversion, edification and eternal salvation. And, seing it is so, we must first renunce Christs authority and dominion, over his Church, before we can refuse and reject that power and authority of the Ministers of the Gospel, who are thus sent by him to us: the truth is, the not receiving of them, is a rejecting of him; a matter that should be tenderly & seriously laid to heart by all; for it draws exceeding deep, upon all sorts of sinners high and low: so that they not depending on any other inferiour authority and power (except that by which they were sent) their obligation to the work of the Gospel cannot be annulled by men. Let us say it, in this we contend not meerly for the ministerial authority, (that for the fountaine and ends thereof should be dear to us) but for the prerogative of Jesus Chist, whose right it is, as King of his Church, to constitute & send Ambassadours in his own name; if there be any thing, that is the proper right of Soveraignity, this is one, which is the native consequent of it, without which it cannot be: shall we allow this, in point of right to earthly Soveraigns, and deny it to Christ, the only Head and High priest of our holy profession?

 Secondly, Moreover, Ministers in this relation they

they stand under to Christ Jesus, have the Gospel & its ordinances committed & intrusted to them, to be dispensed in his name, for the conversion and edification of sinners; for which they are called, the *stewards of the mysteries of God*, 1 Cor. 4: 1. this is a talent they have received from their great Lord and master, of which they must shortly give an account; and which, while they have it, they are commanded in all highest paines to use, for the gaining of sinners to him, in the ways he directs them to in his word. Now let all judge, what a strait Ministers are cast into, in these times: If they forbear on the inhibitions of men, to dispense the Gospel and its ordinances to sinners, thus committed to them, they prove unfaithful to their master, betray their trust, and incurre his heavy displeasure and wrath: If they answer their trust and aime at faithfulness therein, in preaching of the Gospel, and labouring in the work thereof, to gaine sinners, they provock men and expose themselves to all sorts of suffering. But they, knowing the love and terror of the Lord, have on mature consideration of this mater, chosen and purposed, in their master's strength, to venture on the wrath of men; seing they cannot, in this juncture, both please their Master & them; resolveing to prefer the necessity of suffering, to that of sinne, the much commended and cryed-up choise of *Moses*, in the like case, proposed to all in the word for their imitation.

Thirdly, Besides this trust of the Gospel, there is likewise the heavy trust of immortal souls (to whom they are sent) committed to them, of whom they are to give an account, and for whose blood they must answer, when they resigne and give up their steward-

stewardship, and lay down their office and trust at his feet, from whom they received it. Do any think, the threats and inhibitions of men, will discharge them of this trust at their master's hand? If they think so, they shall do well to produce something from him, that will signify so much to them, without which they cannot judge themselves exeemed from the care and oversight of souls; whose blood will cry aloud in the ears of their master, if they do not their part, in what he hath commanded them, for saveing of such. We have heard of nothing yet from our Rulers to satisfy our consciences in this mater, but peremptory lawes and acts, commanding them to obey the same, under great penalties: If we were assured upon clear rational grounds, that their voice and commands were the voice and commands of Christ Jesus, releeving us of this pressing burden of immortal souls, once laid on us, how quickly and cheerfully should we obey their present laws: but nothing can we learne from them or any other, to ascertane us of this. Let any, that hath any true feeling of the natural state of souls, judge, what a cruelty it must be in us, to behold souls perishing throw ignorance, wickednesse, hypocrisy & a Spirit of delusion, in all parts of the Land, while we have the dispensation of the Gospel committed to us, the mean that Christ hath appointed in his house, and useth to bless with power to the salvation of sinners? Will not our neglect, in slighting of this, make us guilty of their blood, and accessory to their eternal perdition? We are assured of this from the word of God. While we reflect and think on this, we dar not, for fear of men and the sufferings that threaten us from them,

them, stand by and look on, but labour, as we can, in our ministerial capacity, to prevent the ruine, we see coming on immortal soules, come of us what will.

If it be granted to us, that our obligation to obey God, in all he hath commanded us in his word, is antecedent and superiour to the tyes on us for obedience to men; and that the commands of men should and ought to give place to the commands of God, (as we expect will not be denied by any, that intertaine the true notion of a God head, much lesse by them that professe subjection to the holy Scriptures, as the only rule of faith and obedience) then our practice cannot be condemned, but must be justified, which is but a necessare consequence of this truth, so universally received and closed with by all men; (except those who have debauched their consciences, throw the predominant love of temporal things, to a slavish subjection to the lusts and sinful commands of others) for are not Ministers commanded to preach the Gospel, and the people to hear it, to assemble and gather themselves together for that end? How many are the commands and precepts of God to us in his word, about this mater? In a thing so clear and evident through the Scriptures, it is astonishing to us to think, that men professing themselves Christians dare issue out commands, so directly opposite to the commands of God, and the obligation on Ministers and Christians to obey Him, before all others. We grant, when there is another duty on foot and called to, *hic & nunc*, the Magistrat may, yea ought to supercede the practice of that, that would hinder the duty, necessare and called to, for the time (to which in the circumstantiat case there is an obligation and
call

(45.)

nt to the Magistrats command:) but to
fix a stated cessation from the practice
led duties, on those, that are under an
serving God, in the maters forbidden
beyond the power of any; to do so, is
state a war with God, and to fix our
sition to him. Are not Ministers and
en in a pussing strait, who must either
, or men? To them that ask us, why
and hear, to the offending of our Ru-
a useing of so much trouble to the Coun-
answer is, God in his word hath com-
to do; they that sustean the relevancy of
but yet deny the consequence, are ob-
e us something, that takes off our ob-
bedience to God, in these things, in
ure we are they are commanded) but
we meet with from the Scriptures of
swer our arguments, and satisfy our
but the cry of hazard from some, and
y from others.

e hold according to the Scripture, that
rat cannot, *jure Magistratico*, exautorat
of the Gospel, or take their power and
em; so he hath no power to untye the
Ministers, and Professors, for obedi-
, in the least of his commands. It is a
politicks, held by all, that no inferiour
annul a power, or hinder its exercise,
diatly derived from, and dependant on
riour, except they show a warrant from
it in this matter it is so: we know all will
Gods supream authority and dominion

is

is superiour to and above all authorities and powers; seing they derive the same from and hold them of him, who is truly *Lord of Lords*, *and King of Kings*. And seing the Ministerial power, as to its being and exercise, in the Church, is immediatly from God, throw his Son Christ Jesus, by positive institution and appointment in his word; no other power can exautorat these, that are cloathed with it, but they must shew a warrant for it from God in the Scriptures; there being no other way, by which God makes known his will to the sons of men; if there be, let it be shown, and this will end the debait, and bring us to a quiet and cheirful subjection to the present laws, about the maters controverted. We meet with confident assertions, but no proofs, without which, we cannot look on our selves, as loosed from the obligations lying on us, to use and exercise the Ministerial power, by vertue of the institutions and commands of God, given anent it in the word. We know the Ministery was institute without a dependance on the Magistrat, and exercised in the Church, not only without, but against his will and command; and God was obeyed, while the Magistrat did countermand & oppose himself thereto, to his outmost; which sayes, that Ministers and professors did not then dreame of a dependance on, and subjection to the Magistrat, in the Maters of God: The truth is, to give the Magistrat a power to dissolve powers institute by God, and to supercede our obedience to him, in the things he hath commanded, is to make him equal with, if not to exalt him above the Almighty God; the only Absolute and Universal Soveraigne of all Creatures in heaven

ven and in earth. Is not this to substitute the Magistrat, and to put him in the place of the *Pope*, that *Anti-christ*, the man of sin, who in nothing so much, as in this, now under debat, exalted himself above all that is called God, or is worshiped, as is prophecied of him, 2 *Thess*: 2. 4? The consequence of this usurped power, now given to, and assumed by the Magistrat, in & over the house of God, is such, that we tremble to think on that, which will (if things continue in this present course) be the issue of it. As we finde, in the accomplishment, that *Luther* did prophecy, in saying that there should arise a *Civil pope* in the Church, who should extend his power over the same, as far as ever the *Ecclesiastical Pope* had done; So we fear, that the troubles, tryals aud persecutions of the Church, shall come near to that hieght, they were at, under the *Pope* of *Rome*. This strange inhansing of things, divine and humane, speaks something to fall out, that will make the present and succeeding generations to tremble; for God will not alwayes be mocked, nor suffer his Glory to be taken from Him.

Sixtly, When we consider the sinful and evil consequences, that would of themselves follow upon our obedience to the Magistrat, in the mater now controverted, we dar not, for all that is dear to us in this world, comply with what is required of us; nor desist from serving of God in the Gospel of his Son; for (1.) If the former reasons, for our non-obedience, do hold and prove concludent, would not our obedience to what is enjoyned us, confirme the unjust usurpations, made on the Church, and wreath the yoke of bondage about her neck, to

the

the enslaveing of the consciences of all, and the losse of her just rights and priviledges, purchased for, and granted to her, by Jesus Christ? As our complyance would have made us accessorie to the Magistrats sin, and brought us under the guilt of all the sin and wickednesse, that hath ensued on the same; so we should not only have been cruel to the Church of God, and the souls of professors therein, but we should have brought the ruine of the Church on our own heads; for not only he that is active in and concurres with the causes of evils, is accessorie to all the bad and evil consequences of them; but also he that labours not in his capacitie and station to hinder them, when it is in his power to do: having therefore nothing left us and within our reach, to withstand these usurpations and corruptions, under which the Church now groans, and by which she is in hazard to be destroyed, but the Gospel of Christ, that we find yet commited to us; we dar not give over preaching and hearing of the same, which the Church in all ages hath found to be the power of God to her preservation, and recovery in evil times. (2.) While we think on the following ages, and the obligations that are on us, for transmiting the Gospel to them, in its purity and power, (as our worthy predecessours did before us) & what are the means and wayes, prescribed to us in the word, for effecting of this great good; and with what successe these have been essayed, in the former generations of the Church, to the benefite of succeeding times; we finde ourself straitly tyed, both against positive complyance with what is required of us, and the omission of that, which God hath commanded,

manded, and put within our power, for refisting of these evils; which if yeelded to and not withstood, would bring our children, and theirs after them, into the darknefs of ignorance, Idolatrie, superstition and prophannefs, from which God in a great meafure delivered us. We dar have no hand in the blood of our children, or thofe, that are comeing after us; which we know, the neglect of thefe means, that are appointed for propagating the Gofpel, would bring upon us, and make us accefforie to. It is not unknown, what advance and progreffe these times have made in the foresaid evils, since *Prelacy* reentered amongst us; and what furder length they would have gone, if it had not been for the obstruction, they have met with, from the Gofpel preached, by a perfecuted and defpifed hand full, in whom the foolishnes of preaching hath been the wisdom and the power of God, to the falvation of this Church. (3.) Although the folemne tyes, and obligations of the Covenants, under which thefe nations once came, be decryed, and all endeavours ufed, that are within the reach of thefe Lands, to difannul, difgrace, and make them void; yet finding, on the exactest fearch we have made, that they remaine in force on us, and this Church, either to the duties contained in them, or els to the Judgments and plagues denunced in the Word of God against Covenant breakers; we cannot to any thing that will bring us under fo hainous and land-deftroying fins, as Covenant breaking and perjurie; which we cannot evite, if either we comply with the corruptions, ejected by thefe Covenants out of this Church; or do not, in our ftations and capacities, according to

D our

our power actively withstand and oppose the same; and labour not for the preservation and advancement of the doctrine, worship and government of this Church, as it was at our taking on of these obligations; which binde us not only to Negatives, or non-complyances with the ejected corruptions; but to endeavour the preservation of these concerns, in our capacities, according to our power. Albeit this seem light to others, yet it is not so to us; for till the mater of these Covenants be disproved, from the Word of God, and made to appear to be unrighteous, antecedent to the Lawes of men, (which none hath yet done) we must judge our selves bound by them to the observation of all they containe, in this present case of the Church. We may not, so far as our knowledge leads us, have any hand in furdering, and advanceing of the ejected corruptions, whether in doctrine, worship or government; but must of necessitie, set our selves, in our stations against them; lest we be partakers of other mens sins, and consequently of the plagues, that God hath threatned, in his word against them.

We shall consider next, some of these *exceptions*, most commonly used against us, with which we are publickly and privately branded, and stigmatized, for rendering us odious and hateful to all. *Exception*. 1. That we refuse to give that obedience to the Magistrat, his lawes, and commands, that under the paine of damnation, is enjoyned to all subjects, in the Word of God? *Answer*. Because this is the constant cry of our opposers, and given for the ground of these reproaches of disloyalty, rebellion & sedition, so unjustly cast upon us; we therefore most

earnestly

earneftly beg of all, they'l weigh impartially the following *Anſwers*, in the ballances of truth and Juſtice.

   Firſt, As we chearfullie grant Magiſtracy to be the Ordinance of God, and by divine inſtitution, to be immediatly derived from him; by vertue of which, all, eſpecially Chriſtians, are bound to ſubject themſelvs to thoſe cloathed therewith, and to obey them in all their lawful and juſt commands; ſo we complean of no little injuſtice done to us, by our adverſaries, who for our non-obedience to the preſent lawes about *prelacy*, do charge us, with being enemies to Magiſtracy, and diſloyal to them, that are now inveſted therewith; contrare to our known doctrine anent this mater, preſented to the world, in our publict Confeſſions of faith, yet extant amongſt us, and our conſtant practiſe conforme thereto. If ſimple non-obedience, in ſome particulars, that greive the conſcience, be a ſufficient ground for this charge, will not the Confeſſors and Martyrs, in all ages of the Church, be held guilty of diſloyaltie and ſedition, who, for not obeying of Magiſtrats, in their ſinful commands, have ſuffered greivous and hard things? None can on this ground condemne us, but they will be found to juſtify the perſecutors of the Saints, and to condemne them; if our reaſons, for non-obedience in our caſe, were taken from the unlawfulneſs of authority, and our Rulers clame thereto, the charge were moſt juſt; but ſeing they are brought from the ſinfulneſs of the mater commanded, while we acknowledge the authoritie, and grant obedience thereto in all other things, how malicious and unjuſt is the charge? Reproaches & lyes will be found another day a weak covering and an unſafe refuge.

                                                              Secondly,

Secondly, We suppose it will not be denyed to us, that the power of Magistrats is not simply absolute, but several ways bounded and limited; as. (1.) By its own nature, which is properly civil and politick. (2.) By its objects, Truth and Righteousness, to which it is astricted, and beyond which, in its exercise, it cannot, *jure*, go. (3.) By the absolute and universal authority of God and his laws, from which it and other powers are derived, and to which they are subordinat. All these limites are set to Magistracy, which it may not transgress; and beyond which, obedience is not due to these, that are installed in it. By the *first* it is distinguished specifically from other powers, as immediatly fountained in, and descended from God, as it; as the power of Parents, of Husbands, Ministers of Christ, &c. some of which did exist and had being, before Magistracy was in the world. We assert that these powers, being specifically different from Magistracy, and as immediatly derived from God, the Magistrat cannot, *jure*, disannul them, hinder their exercise, nor dissolve the obligations on those vested therewith, to those duties to which they are antecedently bound. It is true, the magistrat hath a power about these powers; but it is only cumulative, and not privative of the same: he is to see, that all do their duties in their several relations & capacities, and that Truth, Righteousness, and Peace be keeped, and flourish amonst them. By the *second* the magistrat is bound up, and tyed to, truth and righteousness, and hath no power to go beyond, far lesse to do contrare to them; they being the essencial objects and ends of magistracy, for the preservation and advance-

vancement of which, it was first institute & brought into the world. By the *third* the magistrat is so subjected to God and subordinated to him, (as all other powers are) that not only the right of precedency, in the mater of authority and obedience thereto, is Gods, and not the magistrats; but the magistrat is that much subjected to his law, as that he hath no *jus*, or power, to command any thing to the contrare: his commands here are nullities, as *a non habente Potestatem*: so that non-obedience in this case is not disobedience to him; but obedience to God: for as God hath not given power to any of his creatures against himself; so in the Collation of the magistratical power and authority, there is an obligation conveyed with it on the persons called thereto, to improve and use the same for him, and the furtherance of obedience from others to his laws; for the magistrats power being of God, makes him the Minister of God, for the good and not the hurt of others. Hence it is evident and beyond disput, with all sober minded men, that the commands of the magistrat, do not binde any subject, where God commands the contrare. Court parasites and flatterers may extend this power of the magistrat, beyond these, who through the love of their worldly interests and lusts, (when favoured and advanced by Rulers) more then from any true respect to their just authority and prerogatives, keep no bounds in their assertions about the magistrats power; but the true markes, and Land marks are set by God himself, and will not be removed, but to the prejudice and ruine of these that labour to overturne them. If we make it not out, (as hath been hinted above) that, that which is
com-

commanded is sinful, and contrare to the commands of the must high God, let us be used with all severity; but noe are is granted to us, all accesse denyed, and every door shut up.

Exception 2. But our adversaries not finding sufficient ground, for the former charge, take them to the actions, done in the times of our late troubles and confusions, charging all that was then done upon our party and their principles. *Ans.* We are confident that, when the carriage & actions of the true Presbyterian party, in relation to the Magistrat, shall be searched after, and known; they will be a sufficient confutation of these malicious Calumnies cast upon us, from this head: we know, for justifying of this charge, all the enormous actions of former times are fathered on our party, and their principles, but contrare to all justice; for we are sure, if the actions of the late preceeding times were duely differenced, and distinguished into their several kindes, & drawn up to their true fountaines & heads, that these of them, that are not justifiable, shall be found to rest on persons and parties of designes, inclinations, and principles different from ours, who for worldly respects and designes, betook themselves to, and sheltered under the wings of the Presbyteran party, while in power and successful (as it useth alwayes to be in such cases:) of these there were different yea contrare sorts; that winding into the favour of leading persons in those times, did climb up to that height of reputation and power, as to influence their counsels and actions, to the committing of several enormities, that we dar not, yea will not justify: but after-alterations gave sufficient discoveries

of

no *Proteus-lyke*, changing into every
ke in with the party, that did for the
ine: let preceeding actions then be diftin-
thofe, that we judge right and refolve to
the native effects and product of our
rinciples (how much foever now mif-
) and thefe that were influenced and
h, by the predominency of perfons and
ferent defigns and principles, in our
d alfo betwixt thofe, that were the
rticular perfons, and not of the party;
twixt thofe ufual infirmities, that men
ftate are incident to, in the beft of acti-
fe groffe and wicked aberrations from
Righteoufnefs, that are but feldome in,
en of honeft intentions, and well in-
ciences: we fay, do us the juftice, thus
former actings, while Presbytery was
prevailing and profperous againft its ad-
d we will quickly wipe off the dirt caft
erfons, that keep no bounds of charity
in their cenfures of the late times: let
confulted (partial as they are) and it
appear, what were the true genuine de-
actions of our party then, and what not;
harge the whole party & their principles,
ead, with all the enormities of thefe
ces rather like a Spirit of bitter malice,
tnefs, fobriety, and judicious love, that
il, without clear rational grounds, the
ent of the Profeffors of Chriftianity. Is
, and beyond all difput evident, what
rians did in oppofeing the change of go-

D 4   vern-

vernment, and all the said practises committed before and after, in relation to it: so as the then prevailing party confided more, in the prelatick and cavilier party, then in the Presbyterian, finding them more truely averse from, and contrare to their designes and ways, then the others? But some alledge, that we did raise & put them in a capacity to do what they did? O how weak is this argueing? If it hold, the holy and righteous God will not escape the censures and imputations of thir men; all the wickedness and mischief done in this world will, by this *medium*, come upon him, as the cause and author of it; from whom they receive all that power, strength, and capacity, that enables them to do wickedly. Shall those that do good to others in educating, supplying, & affording them all necessaries, abused by them to sin and ryotous living, be judged the authors of their wickedness? O folly! If our intended brevity could suffer it, we would make it out from undeniable instances, that the government had not such sure & stedfast friends, as the Presbyterians, who were truely such, and acted according to their professed principles; who stood to it, when others (who are now the only favorits) turned their backs upon it, in going all the length of compliance with the Usurpers, that was required; while the generality of true Presbyterians refused, for which they were discountenanced, and looked upon, as a party that was to be supprest. If persons that speak thus at randome against us, could, by clear *mediums*, knit the practises, they charge upon us, to our professed designs and principles, how would they triumph; but none of these have we yet seen and heard. We know, the

late

late wars are fathered on our party, as the first causers and beginners of it. But groundlesly, as will appear to any, that will be at the paines, to search out the true causes and grounds of them; we are confident that, as any, who is truely unbyassed, comes to the through knowledge of these, they will find our adversaries in the blame, and not our party, who for Religion, liberties, and self preservation, (for all was at the stake) were then forced to armes, throw the insatiable pride and tyranny of the then Prelats; but too much of this. Only we must say, if things now hold on in their present channel, in which they have run these few years past, we doubt not, but many will justify and allow, what once they condemned.

Exception 3. It is with no little confidence asserted by some, that although the Ministerial power be immediatly from Christ, by divine institution; yet, the exercise thereof is from the Magistrat, so that Ministers may not convocat the subjects, preach, and dispense ordinances, without liberty from him ? *Ans.* (1) We desire to know, whence our adversaries have learned this distinction ? Sure not from the word; there is not the least footing for it there; if it be, let it be produced. We know its original from whence it came, that man of sin, the *Pope of Rome* (from whose *Arsenal*, the *All* of the Hierarchy hath been brought; and this among the rest) who for gaine, and fixing of an universal absolute dependance of all upon him; invented this distinction, that was unknown to the Christian world before he arose.

But, (2.) We assert, that the exercise of the

D 5 Ministerial power, is, as much immediatly from Christ, and independant on the Magistrat, as the power it self. *First*, because we finde this power was exercised in the Church, in the primitive times and afterwards, without any dependance on, and acknowledgment of the Magistrat anent the same: this none will get refused. We desire then to know, what it is, that now suspends the exercise of the Ministerial power on the Magistrat, that was not then? Christianity adds no new power or right to the Magistrat, it only qualifies and disposes him, to use his power aright; but gives none that he had not before: for if a heathenish Magistrat should exercise all that power about the Church and her pastours, that is by Scripture allowed to the Christian Magistrat, he should not exceed, nor go beyond the limits of the Magistratical power. As we finde several heathenish magistrats, in the Scriptures, doing a great part of the work ascribed to the Christian magistrat; (as *Cyrus*, *Darius*, *Artaxerxes*, &c.) so they are commended for it. It is to us ridiculous, to say, that the heathenish magistrats power is not *intensive & habitualiter* as great, as the Christian magistrats. 2. All moral power does necessarly include, and hath flowing from it, an obligation to its exercise, if moral and Physical impediments hinder not; it not only gives right to such and such acts, and makes them valide; but it binds the persons cloathed therewith to such acts, so that the omission of them in their season is their sin; for the end of the power tyes the person, that hath it, to intend and seek its accomplishment, in such and such wayes, as is proper to the nature of the power; as might be instanced; but in a mater so clear we forbear. *Thirdly*.

Thirdly, How comes this distinction to be given and made use of, anent the ministerial power, and not anent others, about which the Magistrat may exercise his power also? may not Fathers, Husbands, &c. do the duties proper to their relations, without leave from the Magistrat? if they may, give us a reason why Ministers may not do the duties, proper and specifick to their function, without the magistrat? their power is as immediatly from Christ, and is as little dependent on the magistrat, yea and lesse, then theirs; never one hath undertaken this task, but they, who make the magistrat the fountaine of all power: which is most absurd; seing the magistrat did finde other powers existing and in being before he was.

Fourthly, As the power of ministers is from Christ by divine institution: so they are under an obligation, for its exercise, by divine commands, which the magistrat hath no power to imped, as hath been said. They that are cloathed with the ministerial office, are commanded to exercise it, who, in no place of Scripture, are directed to the magistrat, for his licenfe; If they be, let us see it: no doubt we had heard of it, ere this time, if any such thing were.

Exception 4. There is one exeption used against us among others, and urged with no little vehemency, in the matter of our loyaltie and obedience to Authoritie; to wit, our non-appearance before the Councel, on summonds given out against some of our number, at several occasions; which is held forth to be, and strongly aggravated for a high evidence of our contempt of our Rulers, and the authoritie wherewith they are cloathed: for which up wards of 80. of

Gentlmen

Gentlemen, Ladyes, Ministers and yeomens are intercommuned; and the subjects, under the same penaltyes due to such, inhibited all manner of assistance to, and converse with them. *Ans.* Not likeing to dip into, and discusse the severitie of this sentence of *intercommuning*, passed with such solemnity against us, nor yet to canvasse the legality or illegalitie of it; but leaving it to others, better versed in, and acquainted with our Lawes; we offer the following considerations to all, which we hope will, to the unbyassed, not only alleviat but justify our non-appearance. (1.) Beside what the law of nature hath provided and teaches all men, anent selfpreservation; we suppose, it will not be denyed, but granted to us by all, that, if many of the precepts and examples we have in the word of God, do allow flight to Ministers and Christians from the unjust violence and oppression of Rulers, when it is within their power to decline it; then our non-apperance before the Councel wil not necessarily inferre a contempt of their authority, or any true disloyaltie and disobedience to them: Otherwise Christ Jesus our blessed head, his Apostles and others, will be found as chargeable with this crime, as we; from which all Christians do free them. While we think on these precepts and examples of Christ, his Apostles and Christians, who lived in Scripture times, we cannot avoid these two conclusions, which in despite of all contradiction do make out the former inference, as 1. That passive obedience to the unrighteous decrees and punishments of Rulers, is as undue, as active obedience to their unjust commands: injustice in sentences and punishments, binds no more to submission

mission to these, then unrighteousnes in commands tyes to obedience, where the infliction of such punishments is evitable; for Rulers are not enabled by their authority to injustice more in the one, then they are in the other; and consequently there can be no obligation on their subjects from their authoritie, to give themselves up to their unjust punishments, more then to yeeld obedience to their iniquous commands: & if it were not so, Christ and his Apostles sinned in not giving this obedience: which is most absurd.

Obj. 1. But this is contrarie to the doctrine of many Protestants, who teach that passive obedience is due, and should be given, where active obedience is not?

Ans. 1. We know of no Protestants that teach so, except those who were proselyted into court parasites; it was neither the doctrine nor practice of most Protestants, as is clear from their writings and History. 2. We desire to know of them that thinke otherwise, what this allowed flight is, If it be not a removing of ourselves (when the circumstances of cases permit) from the decrees and sentences of Rulers, appointing us to unjust punishments? which is nothing, but a denying of passive obedience to such sentences. Who can evite this? Some there are who grant this, in sentences that reach the life; but not in sentences that only touch the body and estate, as imprisonments, fines, exile, &c. But give not any iust instances, or sound reason for what they assert.

Concl. 2. Hence also we gather from the foresaid precepts and examples, that non-submission to unjust sentences, when within our power, is not inconsistent with that respect, esteem, love, honour and obedience, which, by vertue of Gods commands

mands, we are bound to give to Rulers; and consequently is no contempt of their authority, nor any true disloyalty; els Christ in allowing himself, and his Apostles in practising this flight, had been contemners of authoritie and disloyal to it: which all Christians assert to be false. Hence it is evident, and will be so to the unprejudged, that if our Opposites fasten not this charge on the mater, they will never be able to do it from our non-appearance simply and abstractedly considered. *Obj.* 2. Our Rulers summonds being properly their commands to us, for our appearance before them, (which is lawful and in its self just) we were bound to have appeared, both on the account of their authority, and the thing commanded? *Ans.* This being the objection of greatest seeming strength, and most used to our reproach, we shall consider it a little, and (1.) Waveing the debate about the nature of summonds, and leaving their native import, use and consequences to Lawyers; We assert, that when the commands of Superiors, (altho lawful in their immediat object or matter) are, in their stated designe, so connected with irreligion, injustice, oppression and unrighteousnes, that they become the engines and means of oppression and violence, or of any thing truely sinful in its self; we say, such commands participat of the nature of their ends, and become unjust: as for instance, when Rulers in order to oppression and persecution, command any subject to witness his knowledge of the Orthodox opinions and practises of such and such persons, the subject in this case ought not to obey such commands; which out of this case and the like, that are abstract from such sinful ends, he not only may, but ought to to obey; or if a master or father should require his servant or son to bring to him such a woman to such a place, they knowing it is for committing of uncleannes with her, they should not obey; which, when without respect to this wicked end, they are bound to do. If this were not a truth, the officers and souldiers, that apprehended Christ and Crucified him, were innocent and blamlesse: which all grant to be false, for it was the injustice of the ends of their lawful Rulers commands in this thing, that made their obedience to them undue and unjust, so that they were truely culpable and guilty of Christs blood, as well as their Rulers. (2.) Supposeing but not granting, the summones to be good & just in themselves; yet it is a Maxime agreed to by all Divines, that where two things morally good, doe tryst in Christians practice, the one of one or two degrees of goodnes, the other of three or foure, that the last should be chosen and preferred to the first: but so it fell out to be in our case. To our thoughts on this matter, it was beyond question, that our non-appearance at these times, to which we were cited, was a greater good (supposing the other to be good, which we do not yeeld) both to the Magistrat, our selves and others, then our appearance could have been; for thereby the Magistrat was withheld from unjust oppression, he should have been guilty of, the Gospel preserved with the people in its purity, much suffering to others prevented &c. while we had no good to expect from our appearance, but a meer act of obedience. (3.) That non-obedience, in some cases and things, to the commands of Rulers, is no true disobedience, as (1.). In things without the Magistrats line and reach,

altho

altho the things commanded be just and good in themselves: suppone the Magistrat should command a person unordained, to preach the Gospel, dispense the Sacraments, &c. this being beyond the Magistrats line, it were no disobedience in any subject, not to obey such commands. (2.) In things contraire to mercy and justice, that one Subject oweth to another, if the Magistrat command either the not doing of these, or the doing of the contrare; not obeying here, is no disobedience. The truth is, if the mater commanded be not just, and, antecedent to the Magistrats commands, not necessare; not obeying is no disobedience; and the reason is, becaus no power can justly crave obedience, when it acts either beyond, or against its true adequat formal object: but of this above. (3.) When Magistrats commands are opposite to Gods, (which hath often fallen out) obedience to God can be no disobedience to the Magistrat. But in our case we undertake to prove, that altho the thing commanded, to wit, appearance, be within the compasse of the Magistrats power, that it was contrare to mercy and justice; yea and things commanded and allowed us of God; which will exeem our non-appearance from disobedience, & consequently from contempt of Authority.

Knowing and being morally certaine, that the unjust violence, designed against us, would have inevitably followed on our appearance, we chused rather to fo bear it, and to use the flight Christ allowes to his servants and people, in the like cases. It is a Maxime in Morals or practical divinty, accorded to by all Divines, that of two penal evils, when the election of them is in our arbitriment, the lesser is

to

to be preferred to the greater: And to any that consider the case, we then had before us, it will be manifest, that flight was much preferable to the severity, we were to expect on appearance; of which we were assured, not only from the standing lawes of the Kingdome, but likwise from the preceeding carriage of our Rulers; who, altho slow and negligent enough in the execution of the lawes against *Papists*, *Quakers*, and other heterodox opinious and wicked practises; yet punctual and strick in puting the law to more then its full execution against us, to which they have been, and are instigated by our enemies, the Prelats, to such a hight of keenness, that if the mater contained in our summonds cannot be made to appear, we are put to answer such interrogatories, and required to give and subscribe such oaths, engadgments and bonds, to which, they know, we cannot without destroying of our principles yeeld; for refuseing of which, many of our party have been cast into prisons, fined, banished, &c.

Thirdly, It had no little influence on us in determining our non-appearance, that the usual legal forme of procedour in judgment, allowed to and used with others, is not observed towards us; from which we could not expect justice, but all severity. On our appearance we have no accuser, often no lybel condescending on, or containing our crimes, with the circumstances; no witnesses produced; but an oath administred to the empannelled, for expiscating of accusations against ourselves and others, and that in crimes made by law capital; and the oaths of these, whom the law calls, *socij criminis*, sustained for valid probation; wayes of procedour condemned by by the law of God and nations, except where the Papists cruelty takes place. And if all these fail, the subscribing of engagments and bonds is proposed & required (as is said above;) on the refusal of which, a prison is the belt we meet with. Let any man of ordinare reason and justice judge, whether appearance before Rulers, who, by following of such methods and wayes in judgment, declare themselves resolved to have at the persons arraigned, whether jure or not; we say, let any judge, whether appearance before such, when it is in their choise to appear or not, be rational and safe; except where the supposed guilty intends by their appearance, to prevent greater severity.

Fourthly, Among other things, that came under consideration with us against this appearance, was the oath *de super inquirendis*, lately framed into a law, and now pressed on us, which (for the reasons formerly given) we dar not take; for besids the severe punishments (as imprisonment, arbitrary fines, exile to forraigne plantations, &c.) we were to look for, for refuseing of this oath; if we take it, we are, contrare to all natural equity, mercy and justice, made the accusers of ourselves and others, contrare to the provision made in the act establishing and imposeing of this oath, which declares that the oath taken by any shall not militat in judgment against the takers of it to such & such penalties therein specified, and yet the mater of their lybel useth to be drawne from it, and if they deny their deposition, an oath is adduced for probation against them: And it is not intelligible by us, how such an oath can be sustained for valide probation against others, and not against

the

the deponent; seing a person's own confession of his crimes is judged sufficient against him, much more should this oath, which necessarly suppons and infers confession, even judicial.

But *Fiftly*, In the next place, the evil consequences, that by our appearance, we were certane, would have redounded to many, made us forbear it; for if we had appeared, we were sure perpetual imprisonment, or exile from our native countrey, had ensued thereon; whereby we should have been put out of a capacity, for labouring the preservation and advancement of the Gospel in this Church, of which we are members, and to which we, as Ministers and Christians, are so straitly tyed and bound; the people should have been robbed of a faithfull Ministery, and the benefite of the word purely dispensed by them; the rod of persecution, now on the back of this Church, should have been more sharpened against the remnant of our party; the people exposed to more shakeing and winnowing temptations, to the endangering of their stedfastnes; our adversaries of all sortes more emboldened to vent & spew out their venemous doctrines, and to carry on their designed defection to a greater hight: all which being more then probable, yea to us morally certane, we durst not do that, which would have opened the door to all these evils. These arguments do suppone, and lean on the unjust oppression, intended and prosecuted against us, which is made out both as to mater & designe, in the precedent and subsequent discourse.

Sixtly, It was never a piece of disloyalty and disobedience to Magistracy even for persons confessedly guilty, to keep themselves from the stroke of the law, to run away from it, and to escape out of prisons, if they could effect it, and consequently not to enter into prisons, when cited thereto, must be as free of disloyalty, especially when the cause, for which any is in hazard thereof, is righteousness, as ours is at this day.

SECT. IV.

Our practice cleared from separation; where it is also proved unlawful, to submit to the Ministry of the Curats.

Exception 5. The ejected Ministers preaching, & dispensing of ordinances, and peoples runing to, and hearing of them, in this manner, and withdrawing from communion with the Church, in the allowed publick ordinances, is separation; which is against the principles and practises of the Presbyterians in foregoing times? *Ans.* because this, in acts of Parliament, publick Sermons, and in Pamphlets, is with great confidence asserted; we shall take it a little into consideration; and see whether the Prelats and their Creatures; or our Ministers and the people adhering to them, be the separatists: a sinful separation, we grant, there is, but who are the Causers of it, and guilty thereof, before God, they or we, let our following answers and reason determine, to which, that they may be more clearly apprehended, we premise. 1. That it is not every sort of separation, that is sinful and evil; some kinds of it are duty and commanded, as our Protestant divines make good against the *Papists*, as *Joseph Hall*, and all that writ on that subject: for it is our part,

to

to separat from sin, and Professors joyning together in it, with which the worship of God comes too often to be vitiated, and polluted: for this we have many precepts and commands in the word *Ephes.* 5: 11. with other Scriptures. 2. To make non-presence, or absence from the meetings of Christians for worship and goverment, sinful separation, there must be *first* a stated habitual absence, *secondly* Such reasons and grounds for it, as will not justify it; for if the absence be not ordinare, it is not esteemed separation; altho the reasons of it be not justifiable *pro hic & nunc:* and albeit the absence be ordinare and habitual, yet if its causes, whether moral or physical, be right and warrantable, it is not sinful separation; for absence from the meetings of Christians in worship or government, is either sinful or not, according to the causes or reasons of it. 3. The grounds that will justify and warrant a withdrawing, in ordinare, from such meetings, must be. (1.) The want of a just authority or right, in those that dispense the ordinances of worship and government: The *Pharisees* question proposed to Christ, Matth. 21:23. did suppone a commonly granted, and received truth, which Christ does not deny, but tacitly yeelds; that they who act publickly in the Church must have a just authority & right so to do: we ought to have some rational convincing evidence of this, & if it be wanting, it will warrant this withdrawing; much more, if its want be positively clear. (2.) Corruptions in the worship of God, so knit to them in their use, that they cannot be used without the use of these corruptions, will also allow a withdrawing from such meetings; as all *in thes* grant. (3.) Sinful cir-

cum-

cumstances, as such places, times, causes, persons &c. That in their connexion with, and respects to things, that are truely sinful and evil, becomes so, *pro hic & nunc*; as fasts, thanksgivings, &c. when observed at such times, and for such Causes, as are evil. (4.) Unsound and heretical doctrine, taught in ordinare, in such meetings, Matth. 24. We grant it is not every error and erronious doctrine, that will justifie a peoples withdrawing, from ordinances, dispensed in the assemblies of the Church, (there being nothing besides that may justly cause it;) but only such as is truely heretical and subversive of the foundations of Religion, Righteousness, & peace. When poison is administred in stead of wholesome food, a people are bound to see to their own safety, that they be not destroyed by that, which was intended for their health. (5) There are some things in the stated case of some times, and other circumstances, that will give sufficient ground for this withdrawing, that will not do it at other times; as in the beginnings of defection, under the contests betwixt the orthodox and unsound party, usually some things fall in, that will call for a secession from Church assemblies; which have often fallen out in the Church, and is evident from history; particularly in the time of the *Arminians*, predomining in the Church of *Holland*; and many others that are to be seen in the records of the Church. 4. Although in some cases, a negative separation be lawful and right, where a positive is not; yet in some cases, a positive separation is lawful and duty: it is hard to determine of cases in this matter, except where the case hath been, or els is existent; there are two cases in which this is allowed; intrusion, and an universal defection of the worship and government of the Church, with superstition, idolatry and tyranny, to the polluting of all its ordinances: we hope there will be no controversy anent the second, seing it is the doctrine, and hath been the practice, of the reformed Churches, in their secession and departur from the Church of *Rome*, on that very head; who not only withdrew from the communion of that idolatrous Church; but erected themselvs into distinct Churches, with officers and ordinances, conforme to the commands and institution of Christ: and when the mater is seriously and impartially weighted, there will be found, as little ground of controversy about the first; anent which we take these two to be evident truths. (1.) That Churches are not bound to subject to, but to withdraw from these intruded upon them; partly because the just rights of the Church are wronged and taken from her, which all ought to maintaine, and not to quite; & partly because she is enslaved thereby, and subjected to the lusts & tyranny of men, and a preparative laid downe to others for doing of the like, in times coming. (2.) That this intrusion is either on Churches that have bin and are setled in Christs way, with able and faithful Ministers; or else on these that want & are vacant for the time: If it be on Churches that are under the setled inspection of faithful Ministers, they are bound to adhere to these, and not to give place to the intruders, from whom to withdraw, can be no sinful separation; the intruders, and these that fall off to them, are the separatists: if the Church or Churches be without faithful Ministers, they also are obleidged to refuse the intruding Ministers; and if this unjust and violent intrusion on them continue, they are oblidged to provide themselves of Ministers, that under their oversight, they may have and enjoy the benefite of the Gospel and its ordinances, to which by the commands of Christ, and the necessity of the means of eternal life, they are straitly bound; for as unjust intrusion brings nothing with it, to make a people yeeld to the intruders; so it untys no obligation formerly on them, for endeavouring of their setlment with a faithful Ministery. If we thought these, *in thesi*, were questioned by any, we could with great ease make them out to the conviction of all; but taking them for granted, we surcease any further probation. Therefore 5. We desire, it may be also considered, that there is a vast difference betwixt hearing of, and submiting to Ministers, in the exercise of their Ministery, in the general; and doing of these to such and such Ministers: the question betwixt us and our adversaries, is not whether we should hear and submit to Ministers in their Ministery, for this we do not deny; but whether we should hear and submit to these, that were our Ministers & set over us by the holy Ghost, before this change in the Church; or these sent from and thrust in upon us, by the Magistrat and Prelates? It is no little wrong done us by our enemies, who give it out to the world, that we contemne a Ministery & ordinances, and are against hearing; while our practice, declares the contrare to all, and for which we are dayly suffering. We hold that, as it is our duty to withdraw from, and not to subject to the Prelates, and their Creaturs; so it is likwise our duty, to

cleave

cleave to our former Ministers, in hearing of the Gospel, and receiveing of ordinances from them, as we can, & have access: we have given reasons for the affirmative, & shall, the Lord willing, do the like for the negative. 6. It would also be adverted, that there is a great difference, betwixt a Churches bringing in, and carrying on of a defection willingly, in a Church way; and the Magistrats doing this of himself, without the Church, yea forcibly, *Ecclesia renitente ac reclamante*; although there should be no difference, as to the mater; yet there is much as to the maner and way, to influence, regulat and diversifie ministers and Christians carriage under them: all in the Church are to subject to the power, proper and peculiar to her, which they ought not to do to others, usurping this power, and taking it out of her hands. 7. In this mater a difference or distinction is to be made, betwixt the personal scandals and corruptions in ministers walk, and administration of holy things; and these that may be, or are found in the way of their entry, which may be such, that although they do not invalidate their ministerie, in their dispensing of the word and its ordinances, to the rendering of these nullities; yet may give sufficient ground to peoples withdrawing from and not subjecting to them, as their lawful and sent pastours. 8. There is a great difference betwixt a Church regularly constitute according to the Word of God, in her ministerial political being, enjoying the exercise of all ordinances in purity, that comes afterwards, while under that constitution, to be intruded upon by the sole power of the Magistrat, and persecuted in officers and members for adhereing to her

consti-

constitution, in opposition to the intruders, and the corruptions brought in upon her by them, against her consent; and a Church declining from her former purity, in doctrine, worship and government, abuseing her power to the bringing in and furthering of the said defection, and universally concurred with, and submitted to in the same. The first is our case, & concerns the state of the question betwixt us and our opposites, in the charge of separation they lay on us.

The question then betwixt us, and our adversaries, is not whether we may lawfully separat from publick ordinances, for the corruptions and personal miscarriages of fellow-worshipers, whether ministers or others; as one in a little *manuscript* doeth maliciously or ignorantly state it: we are still of the same minde with our worthy predecessours in their debats against the *Brownists* and *Separatists*; as our practice this day doeth confirme, in our assemblies and meetings for worship, differing in nothing, as to this, from what it was before. Neither is it, whether it be simply or in it self sinful, to hear & receive ordinances from these, who have entered by, & submitted to the *prelates*, abstract from our present case; for we grant the case may be, in which it is lawful yea duty to hear, and receive ordinances from such; yea and hath been. But the true state of the question, is, whether a Church or Churches constitute according to the rules of the word, provided and settled with ministers, regularly called and submited to, should yeeld to the Magistrats and Prelates, violently ejecting their ministers, and thrusting-in other ministers upon her, not only without, but against her consent; in subjecting to such, hearing and aud receiving of ordinances from them; while the Magiſtrat does all this, for furthering and perfecting a courſe of defection, contrare to ſolemne Covenants and oaths, by which they were oftener then once, ejected and caſt out of this Church? To this we *anſwer* negatively; that the Church should not ſubject to ſuch in hearing, and receiving of ordinances from them, but ought to diſowne, and withdraw from theſe, thus entered into the Church, and complying with the introduced corruptions.

This concluſion we prove thus. *Firſt*, They who have no juſt authority, nor right to officiat fixedly in this Church, as the proper paſtores of it, ought not to be received, but withdrawne from: But the Prelates and their adherents, the *Curates*, have no juſt authority nor right to officiat in this Church, as her proper paſtours: Therefore they ought not to be received but withdrawne from. It is expected, they will not deny the *firſt propoſition*: all the debate will be about the *ſecond*, which we make out thus. They who have entered into, and do officiat fixedly in this Church, without her authority and conſent, have no juſt authority and right ſo to do: but the Prelates and their Curats have entered into this Church, and do officiat therein, without her authority and conſent: therefore they have not juſt authority, &c. The *firſt propoſition* is clear, and we ſuppoſe will not be gain-ſaid by our Antagoniſts; ſeing the power of miſſion, of calling and ſending of ordinare fixed paſtours, is only in the Church, and not in any other, as all Divines do aſſert. The *Second* is evident from maters of fact: for there was no Church judicatory called or convocated, for bringing of the Prelats into this

Church;

Church; all was done immediatly by the King & acts of Parliament, without the Church (she being by violence disenabled to meet in her officers for fear of opposition from them;) a practice wanting a precedent in this and (for any thing we know) in all other Churches. *Object.* 1. But our Prelats were consecrat by the Prelats of the Church of *England*? *Ans.* What signifies that to the Church of *Scotland*, and their just right to officiat in her (suppone the office of prelacie were right and institute?) Does any think, the Church of *England* would acknowledge the authority of Prelats consecrat here, and subject to the same, if all were done not only without but against her consent; we suppose not. Either the Church of *Scotland*, at that time, had no power of mission, or els she had; if she had none, wanting prelacy, then our Ministers were no Ministers of Christ Jesus, and all ordinances dispensed in her for many years were nullities; which some of our adversaries, we hope, will not say: if she had the power of mission, how came she to be neglected and usurped upon by another Church, to whom she was not subordinate? *Object.* 2. But Presbyters cannot consecrat Bishops, they being an inferior order. *Ans.* if it could be shown from Scripture, that Bishops are not only an Order and office different from Presbyters; but that they have a different ordination to their office, from that of Presbyters, it would say much; but nothing of this can be made to appear from the Word of God. But. 2. We ask whether consecration be different from ordination? If it be one with the same, why may not Presbyters consecrat? and if they may ordaine (as we undertake to

make

make out from Scripture and Antiquitie) what necessitie was there for going to *England* for it, seing it might have been done by the Presbyters of this Church? If consecration differ from ordination, sure it is a humane custome and invention, for which we have nothing in the Scriptures and pure Antiquity, that only speaks of ordination, the only way, in which all Pastors entered into the pastoral office. 3. The truth is, as a Church Ministerial and politick, constitute according to the Word of God, with all officers of divine appointment, hath the full power of the keys of the kingdome of God; so there is no sort of officer, necessare by divine institution to her edification, but she is enabled, to furnish her self with such, without a necessitie of seeking to other Churches for them: and if it be so, the Presbyters of this Church, being her representatives, their consent should have been had. Although we had no just exception against the office of the Prelates, as it is constitute and declared by law (as we have) but their violent intrusion in this Church, it puts a sufficient bar on our subjection to them, so that we may not, yea cannot owne them as the lawful pastors of this Church. *Obj.* 3. The Magistrat consented to and procured their consecration? *Ans.* If any will make it appear, that the Magistrat is the Church (as *Erastus* does insolently assert without all probation) yea a member of it, as such, or hath the power of mission, we shall yeeld the cause and quietly submit: but when we search into the Scripture, we find the Magistrat, as a Professor of Christianity a member of the Church without all Church power (let be to be the fountaine of it) and subjected as such to the care and oversight of Church Officers, in the exercise of their ministerial authority and power. We grant, it is his part to put the Ministers of the Church (when negligent in furnishing of her with officers) to their duty ament it; but not to thrust in officers upon her of himself without her consent. *Obj.* 4. But the Curats have entered by the Church? *Ans.* 1. This we deny: the contrare is clear from constant practice; for the Curats come in upon congregations only by the Bishop and Patron, who are not the Church, nor have any power from her for what they do, in this: all their right and power is founded upon, and derived from the supremacy, and acts of Parliament, and not from the Church; in which the Bishop acts as the Kings delegat and substitute, only impowered thereto by his law: so that the Curats having and deriving all their power from the Prelates, cannot have the same from the Church; none gives what he hath not. But. 2. The prelates, not being the lawful governing Church, any that enter congregations by them, cannot be said to enter by the Church; no more then if a Minister should enter into a congregation of this Church by a Minister or Ministers of the Church of *France*, or *Holland*, without the Ministers of this Church, can be said to enter by the Church here; for the Ministers of other Churches are not the governing Church of this Church. The antecedent is to us clear; for as the Prelates have entered without the Church; so the lawful Ministerial ruling Church, although scattered and persecuted, is yet existent and in being, who by the unjust and violent intrusion of others, have not lost their right of ruleing this Church; but

in

in point of right and obligation do continue to be her lawful paftours; for violence, perfecution and intrufion, do not diffolve the relation betwixt the Church and her Paftours, either general or particular; there being nothing in our cafe, that can juftly do it; other wayes, it should be in the power of the Magiftrat, to undo and deftroy the political Minifterial Church, both formally and effectively which is abfurd. We ask at any, who think perfecution and intrufion do in our cafe annul the paftoral relation betwixt Minifters and Churches; whether the Magiftrats violent ejecting of Minifters, and puting of *Mahumetan* or *Popish Priefts* in their roomes, will difcharge Minifters and Congregations of their obligations to one another? if they think not, then how can thefe untye their obligations, in our cafe? We ask a reafon. If they judge perfecution and intrufion by the Magiftrat in this cafe, to have this effect; then it will inevitably follow, that the Magiftrat can deftroy divine commands flowing there from, contrare to the practice of divine relations, & obligations to the obedience of the Church, in the primitive times, who, notwithftanding of the Magiftrats Edicts, threatnings, & much actual violence, performed the mutual duties of paftours and flocks.

Arg. 2. All power of the Prelates and their creaturs in the Church is by law fountained in and derived from the Magiftrat, and in its exercife fubordinated to him; (as is evident from the *act of reftitution. Parl. Carol.* 2. 1. *Sef.* 2. *Act.* 1.) which derivation and fubordination they owne and homologat, by their compliance with what the law does require, in order to it: therefore fuch we cannot, we may not

owne,

owne, receive and subject to, as our ministers under seing they acknowledge & subject themselves in their ministery to another head, then Christ Jesus, which by law is set in and over this Church. That the force of this Argument may be more perspicuous and clear, we shall put it into forme thus: Those that receive and derive their Church power from, and are subordinat in its exercise to another head, then Christ Jesus, should not be received and subjected to, as the ministers of Christ in his Church: But the Prelats and their Curats do receive, and derive their Church power from, and are subordinat, in its exercise, to another head then Christ Jesus: therefore they ought not to be received and subjected to, as the ministers of Christ in his Church. We suppose the *first proposition* will not be denyed; all the debate will be in the *Second*, Which we prove thus; These officers in the Church professing themselves such, that derive their Church power from, and are subordinat, in its exercise, to a power truely Architectonick and supream in the Church, beside Christ, doe derive their power from and are subordnat in its exercise to another head, then Christ Jesus: But so it is, that the Prelates and their creaturs, do derive their Church power from, and are subordinat in its exercise to a power truely Architectonick and supream in the Church, beside Christ; therefore the Prelates and their Curates do derive their power from, and are subordinat in its exercise to another head, then Christ. The *major proposition* is evident: for whoever hath a supream Architectonick power, in and over the Church, must be an head to the same, and the fountaine of all Church power: it is a repugnancy

nancy to be supream, & have an Architectonick power, and not to be the head of that Society, to which any is such. Now to the *Minor*, that the Prelats and their Curats have their power from, and in its exercise are subjected to a supream Architectonick power, is beyond dispute clear, from the *act of restitution*, formerly mentioned, and other acts to be mentioned afterwards; and will be so to any that consideratly peruse the same; of which we are to speak at more large, under the last head; but for the time, we propose these three from these acts, for making out of this argument. 1. They are expresly made to have a dependance upon and subordination to the King, as supream to them, in their Church judicatories and administrations. 2. The government of the Church, in its ordering and disposeing, is annexed to the crowne, as one royal prerogative thereof, which not only suppons the government to be in him, as the fountaine thereof, but to be exercised with that dominion, that is suteable to his regality. 3. The giving of Church power to Church officers, is supponed to be the effect and deed of his lawes, and acts, without which, all power in the Church is declared to be null and void. *Objec.* Although the Kings Majesty be supream governour in all causes, and over all persons Ecclesiastical; yet he is not head to and of the Church? *Ans.* If he be supream governour in such causes and over such persons, *in Linea directa*, no question, he is the head political to the Church; for GOVERNOUR & HEAD are equipollent terms: whosoever is supream Governour to any society, in this sense, is a proper political head to it; it is needless to quarrel about words, if the thing be granted. And

F that

that this subordination or supremacy is direct, or *in Linea directa*, is, we judge, clear from the fore mentioned acts, seing they not only make the King the fountaine of Church power ; but moreover in the *act anent the the National Synod*, he is made the *All* of the same, and without him, it is nothing. The like of these, the sun never shined on, except these made by King *Henry* the 8. of *England*; which being scrupuled at by all sorts of persons, at home & abroad, they were, in Queen *Elizabeths* time, forced to alleviat the mater by removeing the title *head*, and some mitigating explications allowed, and ordered to be given to the subjects, at the taking of the oath of supremacy; but no such explications allowed here.

Arg. 3. If the Ministers and Churches required by law to receive and submit to the Prelats, and their Curats thus thrust in upon them, were constitut and setled in Chrifts way, as Pastors and flocks, in the just possession and actual use of all ordinances, conforme to the rules of the word; then it is no sinful separation, for Churches, in adhering to their Ministers, not to receive nor submit to the Prelates and their Curats: But so it is, that the Ministers and Churches required by law to receive and submit to the Prelats and their Curats, thus thrust in upon them, were constitut and setled, in Chrifts way, as Pastors and flocks, in the just possession and actual exercise of all ordinances, conforme to the rules of the word: Therefore it is no sinful separation on their part, not to receive and submit to the Prelats and their Curats, in hearing and receiving of ordinances from them. We suppose, the *consequence* of the *major proposition* is evident, and will not readily be denyed

denyed by any; and if it shall happen to be, we prove it thus. If there be divine obligations on Ministers and their Churches to the performance of the mutual duties of Pastors and flocks; then it can be no sinful separation: for Churches, in adhering to their Ministers, not to receive nor submit to the Prelats and their Curats; But so it is, that the Ministers and Churches, required by law to receive and submit to the Prelats and their Curats, were under divine obligations to the performance of the mutual duties of Pastors and flocks: Therefore it is no sinful separation for Churches not to receive nor submit to the Prelats and their Curats. The *consequence* of the *major proposition* leaneth upon these two, and is infallibly made out by them, *first* that there is a divine relation of Pastor and flock, betwixt Ministers and the Churches, over whom they are set; and *secondly* that they are bound by divine commands, to do the mutual duties of such, contained and prescribed in the word of God: none that acknowledge the Ministery to be an ordinance of divine institution, and the Scriptures to be the rule of religion and righteousness, will be able to refuse these. We conceive none, even of our Antagonists, will deny the *Minor*; if they do, will it not follow that the Church of *Scotland*, before and at the Prelats introduction, was no Ministerial political Church? which is false; as we undertake to prove; when ever our opposites give their reasons to the contrare. But we know the greatest debate will be about the *Minor proposition* of the first argument, to wit, that Ministers and Churches, required by law to receive and submit to the Prelats and their Curates, were setled in Christs way

F 2

as Pastors and flocks, in the just possession, & actual exercise of all ordinances of divine appointment: This for mater of fact is beyond all denial, for the Churches of Christ in *Scotland*, before and at the Prelates late entry among us, in the Year 1662. were, for the generality of them, furnished with Pastors, and in the possession of all ordinances; The debate then will run upon the *jus* of that constitution, that was existent and in being at the Prelats introduction: against which there is nothing, that can with any colour of reason be objected, but one of these three. *Obj.* 1. Prelacy was wanting in that constitution which it should have had? *Ans.* 1. To the validity of this objection, it must first be made out, that Prelacy, as it is established by law, and in use and exercise, among us, at this day, is of divine right, or an office institute in the word of God; which is not yet done, and for any thing we have yet seen, never will; Let our adversaries in this great debate consider the reasons and exceptions we have given in against it, and answer them: yea, we undertake to prove, that it is not only without, but against the word of God. 2. We ask at the Patrons of Prelacy, whether they judge it essential to the constitution of the Ministerial political Church? If they judge it essential, doth it not necessarily follow, that all the Reformed Churches of *France*, *Holland*, &c. are no ministerial Political Churches; and that all ordinances dispensed in them are Nullities; yea that the Churches of the *vallyes* of *Piemont*, called the *Albigenses*, (which by all historians have their original deduced from the Apostles,) were not such, seing in the confession of all, they never had Prelacy from thei

of Christianity to this day; which is
sense and judgment of our Worthy
ho alwayes esteemed them pure Chur-
ith is, the consequence is so necessare,
f the Prelatical party of the Church of
it no Minister of the reformed Chur-
t among them without reordination;
fix a desperat Schisme between them
ches, while they desire and endeavour
with *Rome*: which speaks out the ten-
principles? If they think Prelacy not
Political Ministerial Church? (as some
nt?) then our Church constitution, as to
was right, our Pastores bound to feed,
submit, hear and receive ordinances
bj. Although Prelacy be not essential to
is usful and necessare to the well being
rial Church? *Ans.* 1. As hath been
e know of no good, to which Prelacy
necessare, that is not easily attainable
rea and is not win at in the reformed
. Then the former obligation on our
his Church must continue; for if Pre-
sential nor necessare to the being of the
urches, the obligation, which flowes
dependant on it, cannot be discontinu-
oduction of Prelacy upon us; it should
ne and strengthen this obligation, in the
ch, then dissolve it. It is, no question, the
this and other consequences of the like
forces the most of the now Prelats, to
absolute and essential necessity of Pre-
urch, against the evidence of Scripture

and

and Antiquity. *Obj.* 2. But what was done in the Year 1662. for the introduction of Prelacy in this Church, was but a repossessing her of it, that had been ejected *An.* 1638? *Ans.* 1. The ejection of Prelacy *Anno* 1638. was but the purgeing of Presbytery from Prelacy, that had been brought in upon it, after Prelacy had been cast off by this Church in her first Reformation of Religion from Popery: It is evident from Histories, the books of discipline first and second, acts of Parlt. Particularly that of the Year 1592. the National Covenant, and the records of the general Assemblies, that with the Reformation of Religion in doctrine and worship, Prelacy was also removed and cast out of this Church, as an high corruption in her government. So that from the Reformation of Religion from Popery, Presbytery had the first possession. It is true, the Bishops that then were, did continue in their bishopricks, and keeped their places in *Parlt.* but without all Church power or jurisdiction, that they had formerly exercised in the times of Popery predomining in this Church; And when their Bishopricks came to vaik thorow death, their places were not filled with others, as formerly had been done, till *Mortons* Regency, who for the legal right of their revenues (which he laboured to enhance for his owne use, and could not legally come at, without some shadow of them) endeavoured to bring them in (of which he repented at his death, as is to be seen in the history of the *Duglasses*) which occasioned a hot contest betwixt him & the Church, at that time, in her assemblies, who stoutly opposed prelacie, and never gave it over, till by law and practice it was wholly cast out of this Church, *Anno* 1592.

ing *James* afterwards falling too much
wordly designs and interests, for faci-
much courted and desired succession to
f *England* (to which Prelacy was then
are) laboured by sinister and subtile
roduction of Prelacy upon the Church,
was most averse therefrom) that he
his designe in this, till he had setled it
1612. and brought it in upon Presby-
lacy not being content with this esta-
l exaltation, it attained to in the fore-
ver ceased working by its impositions,
that hight of usurpation on Church &
ocured its ruine *Anno* 1638. All this is
the preceeding records, particularly
tory, that he must be either an utter
se, or els impudently malicious, that
Do men think, we are such ignorants
as to these things, that we are not able
e vanities and lies of some of that party,
pen to paper, and contradicted all this;
of the *seasonable case*, and others, who
evidence, will maintaine the possessi-
in this Church since the reformation?
g Prelacies possession in this Church
mation (which is notourly fals) till its
Anno 1638. as it was in *England*; yet
ight be proven, it can claime no *jus* or
Church of God, whose concerns can-
ted and proscribed by length of time;
st of the popish heresies, idolatries and
should have nigh as good clame, for
this Church, as Prelacy; and it is like,

F 4   if ever

if ever Popery aime at its restauration, and come any length towards it, in this Church, it will build it self on this foundation, among others; as Prelacy does this day, in the laws establishing it. *Obj.* But the Magistrat bringing in Prelacy, and commanding all to receive and submit to it, (Prelacy being, as some say, a thing indifferent) all should obey? *Ans.* leaving the debat about the Magistrats power to the last head of our discourse, where it shall be considered a little; we say 1. Whatever power the Magistrat hath about the Church, and her concerns as such, it is astricted and subordinated to the Word of God, which the greatest Patrons of *Erastianisme* do yeeld, as *Vedelius*; yea *Erastus* himself, and all of that Sect: hence the Magistrat may not command any thing in the Church, that is contrare to, or without it: and if he do, none are bound to obey such commands, as all Protestants grant: therefore till it be made to appear, that Prelacy is allowed and appointed in the word, our non-obedience or non submission to it, altho commanded by the Magistrat, cannot be justly condemned. It is true, *Stillingfleet* is at much paines to prove it to be indifferent, but on such grounds as shake the foundation of our faith, the perfection of the holy Scriptures; and with so little successe, as we remaine the more confirmed in the contrare: wo were to us, if we had no better grounds for Presbytery, then the strongest pleaders for Prelacy have yet shewed for it. 2. The Magistrat with the subject being under the divine obligations of Covenants and oaths against Prelacy, have no power to command its reception, neither can the subject give the obedience required, without

horrid

horrid sin against God: If in such a case, a power in the Magistrat to do, and command contrare to such divine obligations and engagements, and an obligation on the subject to obey these, be asserted, is there not a door opened to the introduction of any Religion what soever? And a power granted to and established in the Magistrat, to make void all obligation of obedience to God? Which, to us, is terrible to think on. Are not our Antagonists then forced, either to assert this power on the Magistrat; Or els to prove the mater of these Covenants to be sinful and unjust, and consequently not obligatory on this Church? One of these two they must do, before they can expect our obedience to the present lawes anent it. We grant, some of that party have undertaken this task, as to the last; but with so small fruit, that on a serious and impartial perusal of their Argueings about it, we continue more confirmed in the contrare, then before the said perusal: whether this proceeds from our dulness and incapacity to reach their arguments, or the weakness of the same, we leave it to the unbyassed to judge. 3. We assert, that whatever the Magistrat may do, either in causing or dissolveing of Church relations and engagments; yet he cannot do this, immediatly and of himself, but by the Church; and the reason is; as the fixing and establishing of Churches relations and engagments betwixt Ministers and Churches, does arise and flow from Christs institutions and precepts in his word; so the application of these to individuals in the Church, either in causing or dissolveing them, is in the Church, and not in the Magistrat: he may command the Church to act her part in this, but cannot

F 5   do it

do it himself, for the power of calling and mission belongs to the Church, not to the Magistrat; as all Divines ancient and moderne assert, and as, we suppose, is sufficiently proven afterwards.

Arg. 4. The way of the Corats entering into Congregations puts a bar on our subjection to them, that we dar not owne them, for the lawful pastors of this Church: for as their entry is without the Church, and the way that Christ hath setled in his hous for that end, so they have come in on congregations, in wayes, which we judge corrupt, and without all warrant from the Word of God, & the practice of the primitive times: In the search of Scripture, and pure Antiquity, we find, that ordination by Ministers, the election and call of the people, was the way, by which Ministers entered into congregations, and not the institution and collation of the Bishop, nor the presentation of Patrons; which, as they have their pedegry and origination from Popery; (a part of the tyranny of that Hierachy) so they are but late human inventions, derogating from, & vitiating the institutions of Christ about this mater, and that several wayes; as. 1. This way of their entry, by the Bishops institution and collation, does suppone, that their ordination does not sufficiently impower them, to the exercise of the Ministery, without a further licence; which is contrare to the end of ordination, & the nature of the Ministerial power; that, by vertue of its ends and the commands of Christ, does bind the persons invested therewith, to its exercise, without which, he cannot prove faithful to his Master, nor attain the ends of his Ministry, the conversion and edification of sinners. It is true, the Bishops

dominion,

dominion, in subjecting of his Creaturs to him, is strengthened thereby; but it everts the very end and nature of ordination, that, by this device, is only made to give *potentiam remotam*, not *proximam*. 2. The Patrons presentation, as it takes away the peoples right of election and consent, granted them by Christ Jesus; so it suppons ordination to give no right to the maintainance; or, at least, suspends it; (the effect of presentations being, in the grant of all, to give a right to the stipend;) which we assert, according to the word, to be the effect of ones being the Pastour of such a people, who, by divine commands are bound to maintaine him in all outward necessaries for his incouragment in the work, and enabling him to do those duties, both common and special, which he cannot do without it; To say, one is the Pastour of such a congregation; and yet hath not just right to the provided maintinance, is against the commands of Christ, and the practice of the Church in many ages. But, as this is amongst the many other pieces of slivery, unto which men, throw ambition and lust, have subjected the Church of Christ; so the Curats, entering this way, we cannot receive, nor give up ourselves to them, as our guids and Pastours under Christ.

Arg. 5. Many Congregations, into which the Curats are entered, are under a standing obligation to their former Pastours; not only on the account of the pastoral relation betwixt them, but for the engagments they came under to such, in their call and reception of them; which is not dissolved by any thing we have yet seen: sure we are, the Magistrat can not do it: *Obj. Solomon*, for the Crime of Treason

son, Committed by *Abiathar* against the state, banished him from *Jerusalem*, (where the Tabernacle was) and Confined him to *Anathoth*, his owne inheritance, by which he habitually disinabled him, from exercising the priests office: Therefore Magistrats may depose and exautorat the Ministers of the Gospel. *Anf.* How wide and inconcludent is this consequence? it is only said in the text 1. *Kings* 2. 26, 27. that here moved him to *Anathoth*, which is but a Civil sentence. *Obj.* 2. It is said vers 27. that *Solomon* thrust him out from being priest unto the Lord. *Anf. Solomon* did this *confecutive*, and not *formaliter*; it was a necessare consequent of his deserved sentence of banishment, to which he was bound, on the justice of the sentence, to yeeld and submit: a consequent that will necessarlie follow on the deeds of others, to whom our adversaries will not grant the formal power of exautorating of Ministers; suppone a man by smiting, or a physician by administring unwholsome physick, do habitually disinable a Minister to the exercise of his ministrie; will it therefore follow, that he doeth depose him from his ministrie, or hath the formal power of so doing? No wayes. And seing the Scripture is plaine in shewing the accomplishment of the Lords word, spoken against the house of *Elie* by *Samuel*, in removing of *Abiather*, and in him, *Elie's* house, from the High-priest-hood; and also the way how it was done; not by a formal sentence of deprivation devesting *Abiather* of his office, but by a civil sentence of confinement to *Anathoth*, that necessarly removed him from the Tabernacle, and disinabled him to do his office there; why do men contend? But ambition

bition to gaine its designe will keep at any hold, how weak soever. *Obj.* 3. As this deed of *Solomons* did discharge *Abiathar* of his former tyes and obligations, to the exercise of this office in the Tabernacle, and opened a door for bringing in another priest in his roome; so we think the Magistrats sentence now does the same, to the ejected ministers, seing they are bound to submit to civil sentences, and the Church may not want Pastours. *Ans.* Although we yeeld the *Antecedent*, yet we deny the *consequent:* for 1. because the parallel betwixt *Abiathers* case, and ours runeth wyde: because (1.) *Abiathers* sentence was just, his crime deserved it, and much more: but ours is not so; as the preceeding and subsequent reasons make out. 2. *Abiathers* sentence was personal, and terminated on himself only, and did not reach the rest of the preists: ours is against all that do not conforme. 3. His was founded on a civil crime against the State, and person of the King, to wit, treason. Our alledged crime is Ecclesiastick, for not complying with a course of defection from the truth and wayes of Christ, to which we and all stand engaged by solemne Covenants and oaths, which tye us, in our several capacities and stations, to withstand the contrare corruptions, now brought in upon us. (4.) *Abiathers* punishment, to which he was formally sentenced, was purely civil, confinement to such a place: Ours, altho it be partly civil, yet is mostly Ecclesiastick; (which is not within the power of the Magistrat) we are not only robed of our livelyhoods and confined; but inhibited the exercise of our Ministrie, and stated by sentence, in a habitual cessation from the exercise of it, which is truely deprivation. (5.) *Abiathers* sentence and punishment was not inflicted, in a time of defection, and for withstanding of it: ours is passed in such a time, and for resisting of the same, and out of designe, on our Rulers part, to carry on their intended defection. 2. The iniquous commands, sentences and punishments of men (where invincible force is not) does not untye our obligations to God and men; that we by the authority of God are under, for serving of him and others in our day.

Arg. 6. If congregations have a just right and power of electing and calling of their Ministers; then those that come in upon them without this, are not to be esteemed their Pastours, nor to be subjected to as such by congregations, but to be withdrawn from: But here it is so; the Curates have entered on congregations, without this election and call of the people, their just right and priviledge. All the debat will be about the *Antecedent* of the *first proposition*, which to us is clear from Scripture and purest Antiquity, as our orthodox Divines prove against the Papists. All that *Bellarmin* hath to say to this, is the power of the Church to alter and change these and other things of the like nature; the very answer of our adversaries: but how or from what this is made good, is not yet showne us: Antiquity is so clear and full in this, that it is a wonder, that they, who plead so much for prelacy from it, can be able to cast it here: if the Prelacy, controverted among us, had but half of the evidence from Antiquitie, that the peoples right and power of election hath; it had gon far to have determined the question in its behalf, with some that yet stand aloofe from it: this shews, it is

not

not the evidence or inevidence of arguments; that resolves many, anent the debats of these times; but interest and lust that sweys them more, then the love of truth. But more of this afterwards.

Arg. 7. Hearing of, submiting to, & receiving of ordinances from the Curates alone, and not from others, is enjoyned by law, and required as the signe of our compliance with, and subjecting to the present lawes, bringing in and establishing of Prelacy, with other corruptions, which we dare not owne. Hearing, and receiving ordinances from such, hath a twofold bar put upon it to us; an unqualified instrument or object; and the respect that by the law it is made to have to the corruptions obtruded upon this Church, as the signe of our compliance with and subjection to these. The command of God about hearing, does constitut the object and instrument (what and whom) we should hear: As we are not to hear all doctrines, but these that are sound; so we are not to hear and receive all, that pretend to come in Christs name, but these, of whose mission we have some rational evidence; at least against which, we have no just exceptions. This, as to the Curats, is made out by the former arguments. But besides this, the signe appointed and determined by the law, and required of all in this Church, is that they not only withdraw from, and do not hear the ejected and non-conforme Ministers; but that they hear and submit to Ministers, that comply with and enter into this Church, by the Prelates: which to us makes hearing and receiving of ordinances from them, a practical approbation of, and compliance with Prelacy, and other corruptions, contained in
the

the law: for such is the connection between the signe and the thing signified, that he that yeelds to give the signe, doth in all rational construction approve the thing signified. *Obj.* But hearing and receiving is a duty commanded by God, which being so, cannot cease to be such by the Magistrats command enjoyning it? *Ans.* In this answer our Opponents do ordinarly triumph; but to unfold its vanity and insufficiency in this mater, let it be considered. 1. That Gods law in constituting of duty does not only determine the act, but the objects and instruments, about and by which they are to be exercised, & without which they are not duty, nor acts of obedience to God, so that is not the act simply, that is made a duty, but in its respect to such and such objects and instruments: as for instance, praying is a duty, not simply in it self considered; but in its respect to God in his son Christ Jesus, for such and such things, he commands and allows in his word; so it is in hearing, whose object and instrument must be such as is appointed in the word, other ways it is not duty, but in many cases, a positive sin; for the commands of God about hearing, do restrict it, in its objects and instruments, without which, it is not duty; so that we must carefully see, what it is we hear, and whom. Let our adversaries first answer our former arguments, and prove that they are those, whom by the commands of God we are appointed to hear; and we shall yeeld. 2. The thing commanded by the Magistrat, in this case and mater, is not a duty; let them prove it that assert this. We grant, hearing of the Gospel, and receiving of the ordinances, is a duty; but only as it suppons and takes in lawfully called

ent Miniſtery (known to be ſuch,) to
diſpenſation of the word is commited:
, it is a duty to hear the word and receive
om thoſe, that are not ſent, or have no
y to diſpenſe the ſame: the Magiſtrats
his preſent laws, reſtricts hearing of the
:eiving of ordinances to ſuch & ſuch, in-
: as to others; which commands not hav-
ſtruments appointed by God in the per-
this duty, do not enjoyn a duty but a ſin:
1: Prelats & their Curats be Miniſters of
then they are to be heard, & ordinances
ceived from them; for the Miniſterial
to the perſons inveſted therewith. not
preach the word & diſpenſe ordinances,
ir acts valide; but it binds them to the
; and all others to ſubmit to them in the
eir power: as is apparent in all relations,
duties, that the perſons under them owe
; ſo that if Miniſters be bound to pre-
el, and diſpenſe its ordinances, the
ikewiſe be oblidged to hear and receive
m them? *Anſ.* Albeit we should yeeld
d Curats to be Miniſters; to the denying
ey have given and do give to many, too
, by their open avowed perjury, enmi-
oſition to true godlineſs; their renunc-
hriſt for their immediat Supream head,
themſelves to another foraigne Supream
; and their wicked and flagitious lives)
juence will not hold: for. 1. The true
ſeſtion is, whether we should receive &
m, as the lawfully called & appropriat Pa-

G   ſtors

stors of this Church; which for the former and subsequent reasons we deny: And we would gladly see how they will prove it, for although intruders upon the Church be Ministers, yet their intrusion puts a sufficient bar on peoples reception of and submission to them; as we have made out both *in thesi* & *in hypothesi*: wherefore in so far, as hearing & receiving of ordinances from Prelatical Ministers, in our case, is an acknowledgment of this, we refuse it. 2. Peoples obligation to submission to Ministers, does not immediatly flow from the being of the Ministerial power and authority, in those cloathed therewith; there are, besides this, other things that must concur to the causing of this obligation, which, if they be wanting, will make it void, or at least suspend it; as the rational evidence of its being in persons pretending to the Ministery, the removal of just impediments, the Churches call, &c. so that there are somethings either physical or moral, that, if they fall out, will suspend this obligation *in actu secundo*, while it remaines *in actu primo*; as inability of body, just suspension for a time, fundamental heresies, intrusion, &c. now many of these being existent on the part of the Prelats and their Curats, in our present case, we finde ourselves under no divine obligation to hear and receive ordinances from them. We shall not here urge the judgment and practice of our worthy reformers anent the Romish Priests, Jesuits, and others in orders, among them, who sustained the validity of ordinances dispensed by such; and yet held, that they should not be heard, nor ordinances received from them. The instance of the pharisies and the scribes, *Matth.* 23. will not be found to mi-

litat

litat againſt this, till it be made out, that they were intruders, which yet none hath done.

Arg. 8. It is of no little weight to us, when added to the former, that the generality of theſe violently thruſt-in on congregations, are either inſufficient or ſcandalous; (creatures we confeſs fitted for carrying on of the Prelats deſignes, againſt this Church and us) by whom the poor people were, and yet are in hazard, throw Ignorance, Prophanneſs, Atheiſme, and a Spirit of deluſion, abounding in all corners of this Land: who, inſtead of preventing and cureing of the ſame, do rather further and advance theſe Church-deſtroying evils; as we do not make perſonal ſcandal, of it ſelf, a ſufficient ground of withdrawing from ordinances, diſpenſed by a Miniſter, guilty thereof; yet when theſe are found in the carriage of thoſe, whoſe entry is corrupt, and ſuch as cannot be juſtifyed, we cannot but think ourſelves under ſtraiter tyes to be ware of, and fly from ſuch: partly becauſe of the little or no ground we have to expect any ſpiritual advantage from their adminiſtration of holy things: and partly for the precepts we find in the word for avoiding and ſhaning of ſuch *Philip.* 3. with many others. Shall we give up ourſelvs to the guidance and conduct of ſuch, in the wayes of life, having nothing to engadge us thereto, but the meer pleaſure and will of men, who, we know, are carrying on corrupt deſignes, tending to the overthrow of Religion in its purity & power? What a folly and madneſs were this? It is ſaid, that our charge, in this, is falſe and unjuſt. But we appeal to the experience and obſervation of the generality of Profeſſours in this Church, good and bad,

G 2   who

who have been & are witnesses to their deportments.

Arg 9 Besides these there were several things, in the stated case of the time, and the circumstances of it, that withheld, and yet withhold us, from subjecting to the prelates and their curates; which we wish were laid to heart by all as they are concerned. As 1. For making way to the introduction of prelacy, the very foundations of civil government were shaken and unhinged, by the disannullig and rescinding of such a series of Parliaments, for many years, in the most of which, there were, according to ancient customes and lawes, all that, amongst us, is held and reputed essential to the Constitution of Parliaments. By this deed not only the Constitution of former Parliaments are struck at; but (as is to be seen in the reasons given for it, in the *act rescissorie*) a preparative is made, for the changing of the Government, by any that, in after ages, have a minde for, and power to effect it. Although the Parliament of *England*, at that time, was as highly prelatical, and as much made for the Kings designes, as ours; yet they forbore such a deed, anent the Long-lived-Parliament, albeit they had the same reasons and grounds for it, that we pretended. 2. This change made in the Church, was accompanied, and yet is, with such a speat of enimity at, and opposition to true godlines, in its necessare exercises; that the persons that favoured any thing of Religion, sobriety and conscience, came under a cloud, and were discountenanced, even from the highest to the lowest, as persons not fit to be intrusted in any place of office or power: while these that were known to be of dissolute lives, and given to all sorts of wickednes,

were

were much made of, countenanced and intrusted, as the only confidents of the time; from whence it came to pass, that wickedness and prophanity finding it self encouraged, and reyns loosed to it, abounded in all parts of the land, to the grief of the truely godly, and the great scandal of the Protestant reformed religion at home and abroad. If it were not for too much prolixity, this might be made to appear from a multitude of undenyable, but lamentable instances; which for brevities sake we forbear, not loveing to stir in this filthy puddle. 3. As to the Government of the Church in particular, the case was wholly altered, from that of our worthie Predecessors, in the former Prelats time: for, as prelacy was then subtilly brought in upon them, by degrees, and not all at once; so they continued in the possession of the Government of the Church, that had been setled by law, and never legally or actually disinabled to meet, and exercise the same, in their fixed and ordinare judicatories: but continuing as formerly in Presbyterated meetings, had the Prelats thrust in upon them; as is evident from history, even of *Spotiswood*; But in our case, Prelacy is at the first raised by law to its greatest height; Presbytery discharged, cashiered and ejected out of this Church; all lawes for it, either in late or former times, being disanulled and abrogated; the meetings of Ministers in their fixed Presbyterial and Synodical assemblies inhibited, under severe penalties by acts of Councel, which became so universally obeyed, that Presbytery had neither a legal nor actual being, in the time that Prelacy was erected & brought in upon this Church: So that at its actual introduction, we were, conforme to

G 3 lawes,

Lawes, required to come in, submit to, and concur with the government setled by them, which was purely Prelatical and *Erastian*. They that deny this must contradict the law, and make the lawmakers liars, if the laws and actings conforme thereto have any sense, that may be rationallie deduced therefrom. Hence, what was required was directly contrare to our principles & known judgment, which to this day, we never saw any convincing reasons, to make us relinquish, Here we cannot, but complean of the valuable injustice, done us by the Author of the *seasonable case* (falsly so called) who contrare to all evidence, makes the case now and then alike. But notorious lies and untruths must be made use of to fill up the roome of truth, so shamefully deserted by that party. 4. The government of the Church that then was, was by law totally subverted, and Prelacy brought in its place, at and by the meer authority of the King; the government thereof by a preceeding law or act being wholly put into his hands, (the authority of Parliament interposed afterwards for the establishing of prelacy, being by this only corroborative and precarious;) as if it were only of his frameing and making, and had no higher derivation, but that of humane authority; which we look upon, as an high derogation of the Regal and Supream authority of Christ Jesus, the alone Head and King of his Church; and a dreadfull presumption in changing the laws and ordinances, enacted and instituted by Him in his house; which all Christians, especially Protestants, esteem sacred and inviolable. Can we, according to the principles we have received and drunk in, from the word of

the

the liveing God, allow of this forme of Government, this way introduced into the Church? Those that love ease, and things of this world, may think light of all; but it is not so to us, who are, through grace, resolved to owne no other Head of that body, (then Christ Jesus) of whom we professe ourselves members. The recent and fresh memory of the National and Solemne League and Covenants; under the tye of which this Nation and Church came oftener then once; all rankes and degrees of persons, Noble and Ignoble, from the Kings Majesty to the lowest Subject, being solemnly engadged thereby against the evils and corruptions ejected by them. The obligation of which had been enforced, and legally secured by a continued series of lawes and practises, for a long time, that seemed to promise all imaginable securitie, to the work of Reformation, against the outmost assaults of its adversaries: nothing was left undone, that could be attempted by rational men in this case. While all these things were in being, and recent in the memory of all, at home and abroad, at one dash, in so little a time, to raze to the foundations, all the former superstructure, and build up the contrare; and that by persons, who, (for their generality) had been so active for, and so deeply engadged in former proceedings, is strange to think on; especially considering the verbal securities, and engagments made unto us, immediatly before this change. We say, in this case, to give the concurrence and complyance required, in joyning with and receiving the Prelats and their Creaturs, is, beyond all question, an approving of all that was done contrare to our fixed judgments & these obligations,

G 4 we,

we, with the rest of this Church came under. Let any man of conscience put himself in our case, & suppose our judgment & principles to be his owne; and then let him judge, if he would not finde himself necessitated to carry, in this matter, as we have done.

Obj Some assert that they, never having taken on the personal obligation of the Covenants, are not bound by them; for which they offer irrefragable arguments, but yet see it fit to hold them in. *Ans.* However there are two things we are sure of, *First*, All Ministers, that entered into the Church in the time of Presbytery, were taken engadged for the government of the Church, that then was, in opposition to Prelacy: and in or near the time that Prelacy was a bringing in into this Church, Ministers in many Presbyteries & Synods, declared their resolutions for adhereing to Presbytery, that then was in being, & had been exercised in this Church, for many years preceeding that time; but it is like (as their after carriage did make out) that these are knots they can easily loose; seing they are, able to master & overcome far greater. *Next.* That Church Covenants in the maters of God, which by vertue of divine commands & institutions do antecedently bind, do obleige all in the Church, both in the time or afterwards; and that with this adventitious and supervenient obligation of a Covenant, beside the former. He hath a stout conscience that will get this denyed, it is so evidently manifest from *Deut.* 29: 10. &c. they must be arguments of iron & steell, that will break this Scripture in pieces. These who assert the contrary, shall do well to try their strength, on what the answerer of Mr. *Gilbert Burnets* first *dialogues* hath on this Subject, that have not yet received a reply.

But

But it seems it is a piece of new policy, to make up the weakness of arguments, with big swelling words.

We might here consider a little (if our purposed brevity could permit it) what one, in a certaine *manuscript*, hath undertaken to prove in several propositions: but his mistaking of the question in the second proposition, makes us easy work; it being a truth we do not deny, and in which we close with our predecessours: so that all his citations of ours are to no effect: for we grant that the sin of fellow worshipers is no just ground for withdrawing from publick ordinances, where there is no just exceptions beside; will it from thence follow, that we should submit to and hear the Curates in our present case? we must have other arguments then any he there produceth, before we subject to such: neither is it a sufficient argument, he useth in the 6. proposition; that they are Ministers of Jesus Christ: Suppone it be so, yet the consequence is wide: we aske at them, if they think it lawful to hear and receive ordinances from our ejected and inhibited Ministers? If they do; how comes it that they do not hear our Ministers, but disswade the people from it? If they judge hearing of us unlawful; they must either say that our Ministers are no Ministers; or els that Ministers may be withdrawn from and not heard, although they be Ministers of Christ Jesus: and consequently it will follow from their own opinion, and practice anent us, that there are some things for hearing and receiving of ordinances, from any person, beside there being Ministers of Jesus Christ: Or els the charge of schisme, and separation, will fall as heavy on themselves, for not hearing and receiving of ordi-

nances

nances from our Minifters, as on us. But enough of this. Whoever reads that manufcript, will find it fufficiently anfwered in this short touch, for all his argueings are againft his owne shadow, and miffe the mark he should shoot at.

To shut up this wearyfome and unpleafant fubject; In the laft place, we are charged with all the profanity, wickedness and enormous practices, that are commited, and do, fince the erection of Prelacy, abound in the Land: yea our meetings for worship, (now branded with the anciently odious name of *Conventicles*. with which affemblies of Chriftians in the primitive times were noted, and defigned by their perfecutours) are given out and reprefented to the world, as the caufe inductive to thefe horrid & abominable fcandals, which are boldly afferted to be acted & commited at them, in a paper of greivances, given in from the Diocefan Synod of *Glafgow*, in Prelat *Lightons* time, and prefented to the then Kings Commiffioner, the *Duke* of *Lawderdal*, and the honourable privy Councel, by the *parfon of Glafgow*, Mr. *Arthur Roffe*, and now Prelat of *Argile*, that impudent and viperous Calumniator, who, from the pulpit, & other places, ufeth to father all the fcandals of the time, on our party and their meeting? *Anf.* paffing that Prelats malicious and venemous railings againft us, (as not worthy of our notice) whofe notour and manifeft lies, his bitter invictives, and ill grounded affertions; (which not only fpeaks his heart and tongue to be fet on fire of hell, but renders him diflked and odious to many of his owne party) we fay. 1. From whence came that fearful deluge of all forts of profanity and wickedness, that filled the
Land,

before, at, & after the last erection of Prelacy, and for a considerable time, when there were few or no Conventicles? We have not forgotten, (and we hope, the sober and humble, that mourne for the abominations done in the midst of us, will not) with what a Spirit of impietie Prelacy entered into this Church, and followed it, for a long time: could our meetings for worship (called *Conventicles*) be the cause of these, when they were not, and had not a being? 2. We beg of our opposites, that they will assigne us the cause of the open reigning scandals, found in them that follow not our meetings, but keep and adhere to theirs, especially in the places, where there are no Conventicles; but an universal subjection to Prelacy? That there are such impieties reigning without any control, in these parts, is past all denyal? And what will our adversaries give for the cause of these? Surely they cannot, with any shew of reason, Father them on our meetings. 3. Is it not observeable, yea observed by all, that, in places drowned in ignorance, sin and wickedness, where Conventicles have come, and at this day are in use, a sensible reformation in persons and families hath ensued thereon, and that to the restraining of these scandalous impieties, that prevailed in these bounds before, and the shameing of these that yet live in them: can that be the cause of scandals, that in experience, is alwayes found to be the effectual means of restraining and removing of them? 4. While we cast our eyes about us, to discover the grounds, on which they fix this greivous and heavy charge, it does not appear to us so much as to give the least degree of probability to it; yea, the evidence of the contrare is so clear and full, that

we

we cannot think, our adversaries do beleeve themselves in these and other reproaches, they load us with. Sure we are, they cannot binde this charge on the doctrines we professe, and are preached in our meetings, which are contained in our printed Confessions of faith, long since emited to the world, especially in the Confession of faith, the larger and shorter Catechismes, composed by the Assembly of divines at *West Minster*. We earnestly beg of our Antagonists, that they will give instances, in any of these doctrines, (if they can) that of themselves do tend to licenciousness and profanity? Upon a review of the whole of our doctrine, in its several parts, we cannot pitch upon one, except the doctrine of justification by faith only, throw the alone merits and blood of Christ Iesus, maintained by all protestants, except some, who of late do assert the interest of good works, as a preexistent condition of a sinners justification before God, which yet is not directly and positively done, but by indirect wayes and hints, as is to be seen in Mr *Gilbert Burnets* first dialogues, *Patrick the Pilgrim*, and the Author of the *whole duty of Man*, who resolve a sinners justification before God, in his serious purpose and endeavour of good works, at least, as a preexistent condition of it: which is not only against the doctrine of all protestants till of late (as is to be seen in their writings) but directly against the great Apostle *Paul*, in his Epistles to the *Romans* and *Gallatians*; whose arguments in that mater, when our adversaries have answered them, we shall consider at more length. All the reasons they give for this charge, from the head, are so fully answered by that Apostle in the 6. *Chapter* of the Epistle to the *Romans*,

mans, and 2. to the *Galatians* towards the close, that we judge it needlesse to insist any further on this. We do not charge all of the Prelatical party with this corrupt doctrine; some of them, particularly doctor *Tully*, hath so clearly and soundly asserted and vindicat the doctrine of Protestants in this mater, against the exceptions and arguments of the contrare minded, that he if living deserves thanks from all the Protestant Churches of Christ, in this and other parts of the Christian world: A doctrine that hath been esteemed fundamentall among them, and given as one great characteristick betwixt us and Papists; yea, it hath been looked upon as the note and signe of the *resurgentis aut cadentis ecclesiæ*, as she holds to or departs from the same. We are not so antiprelatical, as not to love truth, wherever we find it, and the assertor thereof for its sake, although differing from us, in some other things. 5. It is thought sufficient ground for this charge, that some, yea many of the persons that come to and haunt our meetings, are found not to be conscientious and Christian in their walk, but flagitious, or, in many of their practises, scandalous? We cannot think our adversaries are serious in this, & do beleeve as they speak, seing. (1) This does fall as heavy, and will, to onlookers, reflect as much, and more, on the objectors themselves, as on us; whose meetings for worship are found to be the sinck of all debauched and profaine persons thorow the Land; can they refuse this? It is like, the foresight of this forced them to say, in their lybel of greivances against us, that the abominations mentioned in one Article, were commited at our meetings, and not by persons present at them; otherwise their assemblies

semblies for worship should have been as chargeable therewith, as ours: but in this our Antagonists are like to the persecutours of the Christians in the primitive times, who charged them for having these or the like abominations committed at their assemblies, as is to be seen in Church Histories. The Lord deliver us from, and rebuke the lying Spirit, that is entered into and possesseth many. (2.) But if the presence of wicked and scandalous persons, at the assemblies of Christians for hearing of the word, and performing of other acts of worship, be sufficient ground for chargeing the wickednesses and impieties of such on them, as the cause inductive to scandals; will not the assemblies, that Christ, his Apostles, Ministers and Christians keeped in all ages, be as lyable to this charge, as we, who excluded none, but admitted all to the hearing of the word, and some other acts of worship; as is manifest from Scripture and History? whatever our adversaries will say for clearing of Christ Jesus, his Apostles, &c. will acquit us. (3.) Do not men know, that in preaching of the Gospel to sinners, we should designe and labour their conversion, as much as the edification of the converted? Is not the Gospel, with which Ministers are intrusted, the mean and power of God to the one, as well as to the other? And seing this is our designe, as it hath been our practice, so it is our resolution, not to exclude any from our assemblies, how wicked soever they have been, or are: Truth is, to charge us and our meetings, with the sinnes and scandals of those that frequent the same, is to reproach the Gospel of Christ, and to Father all the wickednesse of its hearers on it, contrare to its grand designe, which is to save

sinners

ı ſin; and all the miſeries that follow

SECT. V.

eaſons, why the Indulgence *was not accepted.*

t place, we come to the head of the *In-*
ıe not allowing of which, hath been re-
ıs a full evidence of our piviſh, wilful,
oſition to unpeaceableneſs and diſloyalty:
:, when our carriage, in this mater, is
ught upon, and the reaſons that deter-
this refuſal, are weighted in the ballan-
:ɛtuarie; this charge will be found light:
confident, that upon trial, it will ap-
e not againſt, but with all expreſſions of
, ſhall be ready to iɴtertaine, and receive
for the Goſpel its true intereſt, and our
: is conſiſtent with our known principles)
giſtrat ſhall be pleaſed to grant us. We
t, as an unjuſt ſtate of the queſtion, in
which hath been offered by ſome: whe-
agiſtrat, *jure*, may, or have it within
s of his Magiſtratical power, to give
Miniſters and people, for ſerving and
of God in his Son Chriſt Ieſus, accord-
word; this we do not deny, but chear-
that although the exerciſe of Church po-
is properly ſuch, be independent on the
yet the peaceable exerciſe of it is truely
it belongs to him, no doubt, to encourage,

courage, countenance and protect the Church, against all enemies, and to relieve her of oppression when under it: to this he is inpowered, and oblidged, both as a Magistrat and as a Christian. Neither is it with us a question, whether the Magistrat may command Ministers to the duties of their function; nor whether he may exeem them from the hazard of suffering, to which they are obnoxious by law, for their non-conformity; nor yet whether he may confine Ministers, simply and abstractedly considered from our present case (which is only proper to the Magistrat, and not all to the Church.) All these and much more we yeeld to the Magistrat, about persones and maters Ecclesiastical, according to the Word. But the true state of the question to us, is, whether the Magistrat *Jure Magistratico* may of himself and immediatly without the Church, & the previous election of the people, assigne and send Ministers to particular Churches, to take the fixed and pastoral oversight of them; prescribe rules and directions to them, for the exercise of their Ministery; and confine them to the said congregations. The question thus stated being complex, and consisting of several branches, conform to the acts of Councel anent the *indulgence*; we must of necessity (for giving a just accompt of the grounds of our dissatisfaction therewith) speak to them severally, in some assertions with the reasons subjoyned.

Assertion First, The Magistrat, by vertue of his Magistratical power, cannot of himself and immediatly, assigne or send Ministers to particular congregations, to take the pastoral charge and oversight of them. For 1. We finde not in all the Word

of

on positive institution, and supernatural revelation; and therfore not to be governed in wayes and methods of Mens invention, but in these that are revealed by the Holy Scriptures; without which there cannot be a Church; so that she owning her being, constitution, and all to them; there must be some evident proof produced from these, before we can yeeld to any such power in the Magistrat: how long shall we exspect this? (2.) Also, we finde the Church in the possession and exercise of this power, from the times of the Apostles, to the breaking up of the reformation by *Luther*, and others in *Germany*: as is manifest from Scripture and History. We grant, there was for some time, a considerable debate betwixt the *Pope* and the *Emperour* of *Germany*, about the investiture of Bishops; which gave the rise to other Princes claming of the same, & seasing upon it: but what says this to the mission of Ministers, & application of their Ministery to particular congregations? For as Prelacy was the invention of men, and the cause of horrid contentions in Churches and States; so neither it, nor the practices occasioned thereby, can be any regulating precedent for us: besides, in all these contests about investiturs, betwixt the Pope and Princes, the mission of Ministers was never questioned, but alwayes acknowledged, as proper to the Church, and not to the Magistrat; which will be clear to any that will be at paines to read Church History. (3.) The sending of Ministers to particular congregations, is an act of government, purly and formally Ecclesiastical, and not Civil; and therefore incompetent to the Magistrat: Let any consider it, in its causes, mater, object and ends, and they shall finde it so: for the persons sent are Ministers; the work they are sent on, is to preach the Gospel and dispense its ordinances; these they are sent to, are the Churches of Christ; the end for which they are sent to such, is to gather in and perfect the body of Christ; this is *finis operis.* We know of nothing that can be said against this; But that it is not purely Ecclesiastick in the efficient cause? *Ans.* To this we reply, *First,* That all use in morals to sustaine the validity of the Arguments, taken from the nature of the act, to the unduness of it to such, and such causes: for it is by the respect of such acts in morals, to their mater, objects and ends, that the bounds are determined, and set to them in their efficient causes; for instance, if the mater, object & ends of an act be properly civil, it is granted by all, to be undue or incompetent to a Minister of the Gospel; & so of other acts, in their moral specifical distinction, by which, in the law of God, they are alligned & made due to such and such efficients. But *Next,* Upon this reason, it shall be as lawful for the Magistrat to ordaine, and send persons without ordination, to preach the Gospel, which is every way absurd. (4.) The sending of Ministers to preach the Gospel, and to oversee Churches is an act of the potestative mission, (one part of the keyes of the kingdom of God) granted by Christ to his Church, and never to the Magistrat: from no part of the word can it be made

to

(115.)

...hrist hath given this power to the Ma-
...finde it given to the Ministers of the
...th. 16: 19. with several other places
...But, as to the Magistrat, there is al-
...But that this sending of Ministers, is
...lative mission, we hope will not readily
...any do; we ask, whether Ministers
...ongregations, on a special delegation
...more then to others? If they do, then
...from this power of mission in the
...hey go not, on this special delegation,
...n unsent, and are not the Pastours of
...more then of others; and consequently
...obligations upon them to feed these,
...ny other congregation: which is absurd.
...he power of preaching and dispensing
...there is alwayes a special delegation
...to such and such a people, by which
...the Ambassadour & messenger of Christ
...m they are bound to hear and submit to,
...) This act of sending Ministers to con-
...suppons several things, that are beyond
...ognition of the Magistrat, as such; as
...Ministers gifts; the knowledge of the
...e of the congregation; the sutablness or
...of Ministers gifts to such and such a peo-
...to judge and cognosce in these, as the
...ends of this work require; with many
..., which not being granted to the Magi-
...the work, to which these are necessarily
...annot belong to him: for every work,
...d calls any, hath its proper furniture of
...lities, without which, none is to look

H 2　　　　　upon

upon themselves as called thereto. (6.) Some of the great Patrons and zealous Promoters of the Magistrats power in this, and other things belonging to the Church, yeeld, that this power is in, and returns to the Church, when the Magistrat is either heathenish or heretical, as *Vedelius*; yea all are constrained to grant it. How rational this is, and how consistent with their arguments (the force of which is thereby utterly broken) let any judge: we ask, when this power is granted to be in the Church, whether it comes from Christ Iesus, or the Magistrat? (For a derived power it must be:) It cannot be from the Magistrat, who does not willingly part with any of his power; neither does religion robe the Magistrat of his power, nor depose him from his regality, and the prerogative thereof; as Protestants maintaine against the Papists: if it be derived and come from Christ (as it does) we desire to know, what way it is conveyed to her, in this case, and not in the other, when the Magistrat is Christian? As we finde no difference of cases anent this mater given in the word; so we finde the same institutions, precepts and examples therein, by which the Church is impowered and obliged, to exercise this government without the Magistrat, to continue, not only without any restrictions to times & cases, but without any repail. We hear nothing from our adversaries, to answer this, but *ineptia*, foolish rovings. The truth is, their Arguments conclude, with as great force, against all power of government in the Church, under persecuting Magistrats, as Christian: for is there not in this case the erecting of an Empire in an Empire, which our enemies accound ἀούρα[?]ει and anddo not Ministers, and Christians, owe as much subjection to the Magistrat, in the one case, as in the other?

Assertion 2. That the right and power of Election and calling of Ministers to particular congregations, is in the congregations themselves, to whom they are sent, by divine right; and not in the Magistrat: and therefore should not have been assumed by the Magistrat, and taken thus from them. That this power of election of Ministers, is not in the Magistrat, either by divine, humane or Ecclesiastical laws, needs not to be much insisted on, seing Scripture and antiquity, for a thousand years after Christ, gives not the least ground for it. We desire to know from our Antagonists, *Prelats* and *Erastians*, from whence came this power; or who were the givers of it to the Magistrat? When they have condescended on the orginal derivation of this power, and made it out to be just, then we shall consider it; which by none of these parties hath been yet done; except by *Vedelius*: but on such grounds, as give every particular member of the Church as good clame thereto, as he; as will be evident to any that considers his Arguments: for Scripture and antiquity they have none. The first part of the proposition, is that which is most stuck at; The peoples right and power of election, which is denyed by our adversaries: but we thus make it out, as our Divines have done before us. (1.) From Scripture practice and example, *Acts.* 1: 15. to the end, *Chap.* 6. verf. 1. to 9. and 14: verf. 13. where we have Arguments both from the more to the lesse, and from the lesse to the more; which are acknowledged by all, to be concluding Topicks,

H 3   and

and much used in the Scriptures. When our adversaries have the like from Scripture and antiquity, how use they to insult; but poor we must not be allowed this liberty. (2.) It is evident from the constant practice, use and custome of the Church, from the Apostles times, till the *Popes* of *Rome* inhansed and swallowed up all power and priviledges; either in taking them away, or bringing them into an absolute dependance upon them. For this we appeal to the records and histories of the Church, yea to the histories of the Pops, *PLATINA* and others: in many of which, we shall not only finde the uncontrolled use of the peoples election mentioned; but its right justified and defended, and many canons of Councels made for its regulation, and against the encroachments, that were by some made upon it: in a mater so clear, and granted by the adversary, we need not spend time. If any ask us, why we plead antiquity here, and reject it anent Prelacy? Our Answer is, because we finde in this question, as it is stated betwixt us and the adversaries, antiquity full and clear, which it is not in the other: Let the State of the question about Prelacy; as it is now agitated betwixt us, be in every part of it, brought to the pure times of antiquity; and if it can be evidenced & made out, even as to the sole power of ordination & jurisdiction, and superiority of some Ministers over other Ministers of the Gospel; and we shall yeeld the cause and quietly submit: but in the business of the peoples right of election, it is beyond all contradiction clear, even in the confession of our Antagonists. (3.) All relations amongst rational creatures that are not founded on nature, & are free, there is alwayes

wayes requisite mutual consent; from which, as its proper cause and foundation, it does result; as is to be seen in all sorts of such relations. It is not denyed, but yeelded by all, that there is a particular special relation betwixt a Minister and the Congregation, he in ordinate serves: we desire to know, what is the cause or foundation of it, if it be not this? All other relations of this kinde are founded upon consent, and why not this? (4.) The good effects that have come to the Church by the free and voluntar election of the people, where it hath been admited, and in use, confirmes us not a little in this perswasion: we have obseved in universal experience, that not only a more universal and chearful subjection hath been given to the Ministry of those, that entered this way into congregations; but a faithful and able Ministry hath been more generally propagated, to the great advantage of immortal souls: if we may gather the nature of the tree, by the fruit, we cannot say, this is evil; but truly good.

Assertion 3. It belongs not to the Magistrat to prescribe Rules, and give Directions to the Ministers of the Gospel, for regulating the exercise of their Ministry, as is done in this *indulgence*. Our reasons for this, are (1.) We see no precept, institution, and example in all the Scriptures, impowering the Magistrat to this: we hope, none will expect we should receive and subject to a power, that hath no warrant nor foundation in the word; seing all church power owes its descent and derivation from it: our Antagonists themselves grant, that not only the power they ascribe to the Magistrat, is in and from the Scriptures; but the regulation of its exercise,

should

should be conforme thereto; so that there will be no debat about the consequence. The great Patrons of *Erastianisme* plead the instances of *David* and *Solomons* ordering the courses of the *Levits* and the priests, and of other things relating to the worship of God, in the time of the old Testament; but to little purpose: seing they acted therein as Prophets, and at the directions and instructions given from God, by the Prophets; and not as Magistrats; as is clear from the very letter of the Scriptures, in many places, 2 *Chron.* 29: vers. 25. and 35: verf. 15. with others: If the Magistrats of our time, did produce such warrant for what they assume to themselves, and do in this mater, how readily should they be obeyed? But the *Objection* of greatest seeming strength, is that of *Hezekias* practise, keeping of the passeover in the second moneth 2. *Chron.* 30, 2. which conforme to the institution *Exod.* 12, should have been observed in the first moneth? Our *Ans.* to this is, *first*, if this practise be pleaded for a leading example to Magistrats; it will warrant Magistrats to change things institute by God, which, we hope, all will say is absurd. *Obj.* It was but the circumstance of time that he changed? *Ans.* a command or institution makes circumstances, determined by it, as unalterable by men, as the substantials of the ordinance it self: does not this, if it be concludent, impower the Magistrat to change our Sabboth, from the first to the second, or any other day in the week, as he pleaseth? What may not come in at this dore? *Next*, Our satisfying Answer to this is, that what *Hezekiah*, the Princes & Congregation did, they did it, at or by the word of the Lord concerning this alteration, and
not

not of themselves, as is express vers 12. (2.) As it is usual for commissions given to Ambassadors, by those that send them, to containe all necessary instructions, for regulating their carriage, in the discharge of their ambassage; so we finde in the Word of God rules, precepts and directions, given to the Ministers of the Gospel, about the ordering of the worship of God, and the exercise of their Ministery in all its parts; which not only impowers them for this work, but brings them under as strait Obligations to observe the same, as the work and maine substantials of the ambassage, on which they are sent: for this let 1 Cor. 14. two Epistles to *Timothy* with other Scriptures be consulted; and we doubt not but this will be beyond dispute with the unprejudged. If the *Erastians* could give us such commands and precepts in the word, for the Magistrats power in this, how would they triumph, and so they justly might; for they should have no such willing and cheirful assenters to them then we; if any such thing could be shewed. (3.) This power in the Magistrat would subject Ministers to and bring them, in the exercise of their ministerie, in a dependance on him; the contrare of which we have proved before, and shall do more afterwards: The truth is, we tremble to think on the consequences of this dependance; for thereby the Magistrat may suspend the ministry, in these parts and exercises of it, that Christ Jesus cals them to, in the stated cases of the times, in which they live; as for instance, when heresies are abounding, and Professors taken with the infection of that leaven, he may put them on the preaching of doctrines not apposite to the present case, and discharge them from

medling

medling with doctrines contrare to the present errours; as our Magistrats have done anent some doctrines in these times: he may likewise forbid them preaching against, or censuring of these sinnes that are reigning in the place and time, in obeying of which, Ministers shall cross the commands of Christ to them in his word, and bring themselves under the guilt of the blood of soules. If Churches and Ministers be not, in the commands, precepts, and institutions of God, exeemed from the power and impositions of men, what a sad case will they be in? (4.) The Church had and exercised this power from Scripture times in all ages, till within these hundereth years. We grant the Magistrat exercised a power about, or anent the Church; but never came this length: when they did reforme, & gave any redress of corruptions, creept into the administrations of holy things, they did it by the Church; whom, in her officers, they did convocat, and require to consider the mater, and to make constitutions about it; but never essayed to do it immediatly, and by themselves; as Church Histories make evident, beyond all contradiction. (5.) It is the natural right of all moral power, to order and dispose its owne exercise, in and about the Matets that are proper to it; as might be made to appear by instances of these of the Parental, Marital Powers, &c. and the reason is, partly, because the objects and other circumstances are so many and various; that it is not possible to prescribe rules, comprehensive of all particular emergents, relating to their excercise, but must be left to the prudence of those invested with them, to do therein, as they see fit and expedient, in the cases that are before them

and

and partly such are fittest, as having more knowledge and experience about such things, that belongs to their power, then any others. We see this yeelded to others, and why then not to Ministers, who may, in rational judgment, be presumed, to have more solide knowledge and experience, in and about the maters of God, as any? (6.) All divines (except those called *Erastian*, who are but of a late edition in the Church) yea the Prelatical ones, doe grant a *diatactik* power to the Ministery of the Gospel, about the worship and government of the Church, and the exercise of their Ministry relating thereto: and till ERASTUS the phisitian arose, it was beyond controversie among all Church writers, whether Historical or Polemick; even those, who contended for the Magistrats power, against the usurpations of the *Popes*; as is to be seen in their Tractats; from which we might adduce citations not a few; but fearing they wold prove too tedious, if inserted here, We forbeare.

Assertion 4. Albeit we grant, the power of confinement be proper to the Magistrat, and not at all to the Church (for to him only is the sword given, to be used against evil doers;) yet in the complex case, which we had before us, we durst not approve of the *indulgence*, with such a clause; seing we had not (as may be clear to any from what is said above) any other thing, in this mater, to Ingadge us, to an acceptance thereof. For the act of indulgence confines the Ministers of the whole party: if it had been but some few, that this confinment reach'd, we would not have said much to it, although the sentence had been unjust. But while we
consid-

considered the present universal necessity of the Church, and the obligations on us, to use our Ministery, for answering the same, we could not, with quietness to our consciences justifie nor allow of it as a favour, with such a restraint on our Ministry. If the confinment had only touched our persons, and personal concerns, we had with all patience and submission yeelded thereto; but a restraint being put on the exercise of our Ministery, in this necessitous condition of the Church, when *Papists*, *Quakers* and other subverters of truth and godliness, do multiply and abound, without all curb, we could not close with this indulgence; which, by vertue of the confinment, puts us out of capacitie, for affording that relief to the Church and immortal souls, which our office binds us to. (2.) As there are many duties and parts of our Ministerial function, which we cannot performe and exercise, but in a conjunction with others; so this indulgence cuts off from all accesse to the same, and leaves us in much worse case, then we were in before. Have we not the Gospel of Christ to maintaine against its present adversaries? Are we not bound to propagat the same in the present and succeeding ages? Do not scandals of all sorts abound, to the overthrow of truth and piety? and does not the care and burdine of seeing to and providing against the evil, that in these times, threaten the ruine of the Church, lye upon us in our ministerial capacity? And we cannot singly and apart, doe what is necessare in this case, but in a conjunction with one another: no doubt, our subjecting to this confinment would render us accessory to, and bring us under the guilt of all these evil and their consequences

ces to this, and the following generations. Posterity, no question, should have all cause to curse and charge their blood upon us, which is trembling to think upon. (3.) If we may guesse at, and be ascertained of the ends and designes of mens actions, by the native effects and consequences of them; it is to us apparent and beyond denyal, that the project and intention of this contrivance, was quietly to ruine and bury our cause; seing by this confinment, and other things in this *indulgence*, all endeavours towards the succession of a faithful ministery, are cut off, and we brought unto an immediat dependance on the Magistrat, in the maters of God, and hindered to propagat the truth, in opposition to its adversaries, in other parts of the land; being thus shut up into a little corner of the same, & cast by two's & three's and fours, into congregations; where, for the most part, there is little or no use for us; If the Apostles and other Ministers of Christ, in Scripture times, had been thus dealt with, and in policy confined, as we are; do any think, they would have submitted to, and obeyed such a confinment, which would have frustrated the ends of their office and work; and made them guilty of disobedience to their Master, from whom they received commands, inconsistent with such a sentence? And shall we subject and be consentient to a deed, that in the designe and effects thereof will infallibly destroy the cause, which, by all sorts of obligations, we are engadged to maintaine and advance to the utmost of our power? God forbid. We are not ignorant, that the confinment, with a permission to preach and exercise other parts of our ministry, in the places, to which we were to

in

be confined; was a piece of policy, invented to cover the too visible encroachment on Church power, in the first act of Indulgence (which was known afterwards to stumble many) that the mater might be more smoothed, and goe the better down; while the designe was the same; which was (as is said) to bring our ministry in subjection to the Magistrat, in the maters of God; and without noise to obstruct the spreading of the Gospel, and to ruine our cause; for attaining of which, we have not yet seen a more succesful like piece of policy, then this of the *indulgence*.

Resolveing (as hath been said) to unfold our hearts, and to keep nothing up, anent what is truly greivous to, and burdens our consciences, in the commands and impositions of these times; we shall adde other reasons to these, which, with the former, are the grounds of our dissatisfaction with and non-approbation of this *indulgence*: as (1.) In the Narrative of the 2. *act of indulgence*, it is declared, that this pretended favour is provided for a remedy against the evil of Conventicles, (by which we understand the assemblies of the Lords people for hearing of the word, and partaking of other ordinances from faithful Ministers of the Gospel) which the execution of laws made against the same, hath not suppressed. As this narrative speaks to all, the designe of the *indulgence*; so it shews, what we are to expect as its consequence, if approven by us, to which we dar have no accession, directly nor indirectly; for by our allowance, and submission, we shall not only prove active in hindering the propagation of the word for the future; but also shall consequentially condemne

the

actice of the Lords servants and people, and hearing of the word; that hath been made not a little succesful, to the ad-
 truth, and the benefite of many souls.
 y this indulgence were assigned and sent gregations, then these they had formerly Master in, before this revolution in the we judge the former relations to parti-
(ever which the Holy Ghost, and not iad made them overseers) to be yet in not dissolved by all the violence used a-
) we think our approbation of this indul-
ld not only justify the unjust usurpation, in casting them out; but likwise would aid the former, and yet standing relation ective congregations, in which we darre
l, but in the way Christ hath appointed, eerly used in this Church; seing it will, both strengthen the Magistrat, in his achments on the Government of the nd be a practical acknowledgement of
e hath done in this mater. (3.) By one 2, *act of indulgence*, appeals are allowed ed from the indulged to the Prelats iich does subject, and directly subordi.
these, in the exercise of government and which is known, to be contrare to our and well grounded principles. The truth
 on this, with other particulars in that as a device framed of purpose, for gain-
nds and intents upon us, which by vio-
een formerly designed against us, for of *Prelacy* and *Erastianisme*. (4) As
some

some of the Rules are impracticable, so others of them do not a little reflect upon the practises of Christ and his Apostles, recorded by the Evangelists, who preached in houses and fields. If we understand our Christian profession aright, we must take our selves bound by many commands and precepts in the word of God, to imitat Christ and his Apostles, in their performances of the duties of Religion and righteousness, which are of purpose related in the Scripturs for this effect. Do we not find from these sacred records, Christ and his Apostles preaching in houses and fields, as occasions offered, never declining to teach and instruct the people in these, as the present exigence required, although they had the opportunity of and accesse to the Synagogues, which is denyed us, as to the places allowed for publict worship? Do not these practices of Christ and his Apostles say, that, as preaching in houses and fields, is in it self no sinne but lawful; (except we resolve to make Christ a transgressour) so in the like cases, and under the like calls, we are bound to do in this, as Christ did before us; who can get this shuned?

Amongst the many designes aimed at, in this *indulgence*, and in part obtained by it; we know the deviding and breaking of our party, was a principal one; which at first actuated, and set on foot this device amongst us; but, we hope, without the fruit our adversaries expected to have reaped thereby, to the advantage of their cause: for, whatever difference there hath been, or yet is amongst us, in our practice, in relation to the *indulgence*, we are all agreed in the preceeding exceptions against it; and if there had been accesse for representing the same to our

Rulers,

r unanimity and concord in these had
iscovered, and made known to the world,
There is no change with us of our
rofessed judgment, about the Govern-
Church, in its true distinction from, and
on the Magistrat, as is afterward ex-
hat ever was our perswasion in this, re-
the world in our publick confession of
t, throw the grace of God, resolve to
aving never seen or heard of any thing,
es that have gone over our heads, to
our apprehensions of this mater in the
who take hold of all occasions to repro-
leased to represent some their acceptance
ence, as contradictory to, and inconsi-
ur former professed principles anent
ernment: yet any that considers what
hinted at, to the Councel, at the re-
s indulgence; and what was more lar-
by them to the congregations, at their
ill be sufficiently convinced of our con-
e to our former principles; which by
e is not at all changed. It is expected
rs of our righteous cause, that noth-
lone by them, toward the furtherance
nts of this indulgence: but rather an
counteract and ineffectuat them,
sites may have no benefite therefrom,
ce of the interests of Christ, for which

I   SECT.

SECT. VI.

The nature of Church Government, *as distinct from and independent upon Magistracy, explained.*

Having proceeded thus far, and dispatched the first three things, we proposed to speak to, in the beginning, we shall now enter on the last, the *Supremacy Ecclesiastical*, that is now by law annexed to the crown, established in his majesties person and successours, and sensed by law and practice. Let none wonder, we take this ticklish subject into consideration, and dar adventure, to give an accompt of our thoughts of the same, to the world: for we solemnly professe, that on the exactest enquiry and search, that we have been able to make about this mater; we find it, as diametrically opposite to our true Covenanted principles, as Prelacy; and in its effects, we fear shall prove as destructive to the Church, and work of Reformation, as any thing that appeared on the field against it: Times past and present speak much to this, but the future will say more: the storme that this *Supremacy* threatens to this Church and nation, is such, that it is the part of all that wish well to *Zion* to pray instantly day and night, that it may be graciously averted. The truth is, as we look upon it, as an high corruption in it self tending to the subversion of the Churches concerns, in doctrine, worship, and Government; so it lies at the bottome of our non-conformity to the law, in Church maters; and is not only one, but a maine reason, why we

cannot

in Church assemblies, especially for
which thereby, in our apprehensions,
:ies. That our procedour in speaking
be distinct and clear to all, we shall
iethod. 1. We shall consider & speak
ment of the Church, and shew what
We shall prove its distinction from, &
on the civil Government. And 3. Shew
Government of the Church is by law
d exercised by our Rulers, contrare to
the practice of the Church, till these
rs past.
ight to the whole, we shall premise
ary considerations or propositions,
ink, will not readily be denied by any.
is out of our rode, and inconsistent
ded brevity, to insist on the tearms GO-
T & CHURCH, & what is usually sig-
; these we leave to the Criticks and all
his subject: but all are agreed in this,
NMENT is a tearme importing power
; which is nothing els, but a right to
d an obligation on these invested there-
e same, for attaining the ends of Go-
that Government makes its acts due &
erson, or persons cloathed with it; &
o all these acts, means & wayes, by
nment is enabled to reach its ends. 2.
ated power & authority is originall in
irst cheif cause thereof, & derived from
niversal Supreme Monarch, and Go-
n heaven or earth; hence it necessarly
:, as the power that cannot prove its
descent

descent from God, is not to be admitted; so all j[ust]
powers are directly subordinat to him as the univer[sal]
head of all. 3. *Propos.* that the Church of Chr[ist]
not being founded in nature, but on supernatural [re]
velations, her Government must wholly depend up[on]
& flow from it, in these things where it differs fro[m]
other Governments; so that the *All* of this G[o]
vernment is by positive institution and warrant fro[m]
God supernaturally revealed. 4. *Propos.* Th[at]
Christ Jesus, as Mediator, Being made the head [of]
the Church under God; and thereby her Gover[n]
ment fountained in him: all powers in the Chur[ch]
must be derived from, and subordinat to him, as t[he]
Supream. 5. *Propos.* Beside the invisible and i[n]
ternal Government, that Christ Jesus exerciseth b[y]
his Spirit, on the souls and consciences of his peopl[e]
(that consists in the inward light and power of h[is]
Spirit guiding and enabling them to that obedience
he requires of them in his word;) there is likwise [a]
true visible Government of the Church, institute b[y]
him, and visibly exercised in her, in his name, as h[er]
Supream. 6. *Propos.* The Government of the Churc[h]
(as shall be proved afterwards) is not properly, an[d]
in linea directa subordinat to the Magistrat, for 1. [It]
hath its derivation from another fountaine, Chri[st]
Jesus; who being the Churches Supream head an[d]
governour, all power in her must come from and d[e]
pend on him. 2. The Magistrat cannot take away
nor change the Government of the Church, whic[h]
he may do in Governments and powers subordinat [to]
him: yea, he cannot impede its exercise, in these i[t is]
trusted with it; seing they are under obligations f[or]
it, antecedent & superiour to these of the Magistra[t.]
7. *Propo[s.]*

Propof. That the holy Scriptures, being the Word and law of Chrift, as King of his Church, muft be the inftrument and rule of the Churches Government, according to which she ought to be ruled, not only in thefe acts of faith and obedience in the inner Man, but also in the outward. 8. *Propof.* Although Powers fpecifically diftinct be not fubordinat to one another; yet there may be and is a mutual fubordination of perfons, invefted with thefe powers, fo as the perfons are in different refpects fuperiour and inferiour to one another; as *Jeſſe* was to *David* (fuppofing him to live in his fon *Davids* reigne;) which fubordination of perfons does not take away the diftinction of thefe powers; nor the mutual fubjection, the perfons owe to one another: hence we affert, that as Magiftracy does not deftroy the Miniftry, nor depose the perfons cloathed therewith, from the subjection they owe, as Chriftians, to Minifters, in the right exercife of their Miniftery; fo neither does the Miniftery deftroy Magiftracy, nor untye Minifters, as fubjects, from that fubjection and obedience due to Magiftrats from their fubjects; Minifters are bound to this as much as any. 9. *Propof.* As in all Governments, there are fomethings that is intrinfick (although vifible) wherein its nature and fpecifick effence does confift, and fomethings accidental and feparable from it, that belongs not to its *Effe*, but BENE ESSE; fo there are in the vifible Government of the Church, fomethings effential & intrinfick, (of which afterward) and fomethings accidental and extrinfick, without which it can fubfift, even in its exercife. 10. *Propof.* Thefe things, in and about which, the Government of the

I 3 Church

Church is conversant, are of diverse sorts; some purely spiritual, as the Word, Ministery, Sacraments, and all Ordinances of divine appointme[nt] Others are of a mixt nature, partly spiritual & pa[rtly] civil, as the necessary circumstances and mod[es of] worship and Government; which, although c[ivil] in their own nature, and common to other actio[ns] yet partly by reason of the general divine appo[int]ments, impowering the Church to dispose and [or]der these; partly by reason of their necessary con[nex]ion with things purely spiritual, are truely Eccl[e]siastick, and become a part of the object of the p[ro]per power of Church Government, called by all [Di]vines *DIATACTICK*: Some are properly & pur[ely] civil, in their owne nature and immediat ends; [as] Churches, Stipends, Manses, Glybs, &c, whic[h] although they be by general precepts secured to t[he] Church, and belonging to her; yet they are fo[r]mally civil, and come directly under the Magistra[te's] power, as other civil rights and proprieties do, abo[ut] which he does execute the judgment of truth & peac[e.]

11. *Propos.* It is to be adverted, that there is a tw[o]fold subordination of powers in Government; one *LINEA DIRECTA*; and another *in LINEA OB[-]LIQUA*: in the *first* subordination, the power sub[-]ordinated is derived from, and comprehended in t[he] Supream, and may be impeded, suspended or reg[ul]ated in its exercise, yea totally dissolved by it; a[nd] when exercised, it is in the name and authority of t[he] Supream, and wholly dependant, in its regulatio[n] on it; so that both the power as such, the person i[n-] trusted therewith, and its exercise, is subjected [to] the Supream. In the *second* kind of subordinatio[n]

subordinated power, or rather the person in its exercise, is only the object of some acts of another power; but the power is not derived from it, nor impedible or regulable by it: It is in this sort of subordination, that Magistrats and Ministers are subordinated to one another, without all subordination of the powers, in their exercise; for Magistrats may, yea should command Ministers, when negligent, to the duties of their function; so Ministers ought, in Christs name, to command Christian Magistrats to do the duties belonging to their office; and to rebuke them authoritatively, when found acting contrare thereto. 12. *Propos.* These subjected to created powers, whether Magistratical or Ministerial, being under the supream, absolute and universal Soveraignity of God, have a power of judgment and discretion granted to them, for cognoscing on the commands of their superiours, as to their justice or injustice, or their consistency with, or repugnancy to the commands of God; by which they are to walk in giving or not giving obedience to their superiours.

The way being thus paved, our next work is, to shew, what we judge to be the Government of the visible Church, which we shall do in these Conclusions. *Conclus.* 1. The Government of the visible Church largely considered, is either Supream or Subordinat: to the Supream belongs the legislative power, as the making and enacting of lawes, instituting of ordinances, appointing and impowering of officers; and to be the fountaine of all power in the Church. This we assert to be only in Christ Jesus; and visible in his word, ordinances, officers, and the

con-

conveyance of all Church power: in this, none share with him either Magistrats or Ministers. *Conclus.* 2. The subordinat power of Government in the Church, is in her officers, that Christ hath appointed and called thereto; which power, is only and immediatly from Christ, and exercised in his name, over all in the Church, which distinction of Church Government makes not different Governments in the head and members; it being one and the same Government, truly Monarchical, not Aristocratical, nor Democratical. *Concl.* 3. This derived and subordinat power in Church officers, when considered with respect to its mater, in and about which it is exerced, is diverse: Schoolmen and Divines distinguish it, into the *power* of *Order* & *Jurisdiction*; but for explications sake, and avoiding of all ambiguity, we shall consider it, in the variety of its objects or mater; and its divers acts about the same.

As (1.) To it belongs the dispensing of the ordinances of worship, in the publict assemblies of the Church, in preaching of the word, praying to (as the mouth of the assembly) and praising of God: in these they act, as the Authorized servants of Christ, in performing and directing of the worship of God in the Church. (2.) The convocating of the Assemblies of the Church, for these divine and holy exercises; on which all in the Church are bound by divine precepts to attend, as the institute means of worship, conversion, and edification. (3.) The receiving, ordering, and distributing of the Charitable contributions of the Church, for maintaining of the poor, and doing of other pious works. (4. Trying,

ing, receiving, and admitting of members into the Church, confirming and sealing of the same by Baptisme. (5) Administring the great ordinance of the Lords supper, to the worthy and obedient, conforme to the institution of it in the word. (6.) Ejecting and excluding the impenitent and obstinatly scandalous (after due trial and conviction) whether in doctrine or manners, from the Sacraments, and Comunion with the Church in these. (7.) Trying, calling, and ordaning of persons fitted for and willing to engadge in the Ministery; according to the rules of the word. (8.) Deposing and exautorating of Ministers from the Ministery, who, by heresy or scandals, declare themselves unworthy of, and unfit for the same. (9) Trying, and censuring of scandals, in persons found guilty of them (after due conviction) for their recovery, and keeping of the Church pure. (10.) Associating into stated & fixed meetings, for carrying on, and doing of the former and subsequent work, whether more general or particular, in their due and allowed subordination. (11.) Trying and judging of doctrines, whether sound or heretical, according to the rule of the word of Christ, and censuring of persons found unsound in the faith. (12.) Disposing & ordering the necessary circumstances of worship and Government, for decency and order, and the avoiding of confusion. (13.) Resolving of doubts and cases of conscience, incident to the Church, on any occasion or emergent. (14.) Indicting of dayes of publick solemne fasts and humiliation, or of thanksgiving, as the dispensations of judgment and mercy call to the same, &c.

 Conclus. 4. This Government of the Church,

as it is in the hands of Church officers, and exercised by them, is purely Ministerial, without all dominion in them; and only *executive* in applying the will of Christ to the members of the Church, as they are found conform or disconform to the same. *Concl.* 5. This subordinat power in Church officers is only *declarative* and *nuncupative*, and not properly *decisive*; they have not power to determine what shall be true or false doctrine, sin or duty; and what censure shall be inflicted on persons heretical or scandalous; but only to declare and apply the will of Christ, and what he hath determined anent these in his word. This power suppons its object, and does not make it. *Concl.* 6. It is wholly limited, regulated by, and restricted to the word and law of Christ, as its basis and rule, beyond which it cannot go; and if it do, its acts are nullities and not obligatory on any. *Concl.* 7. It is purely spiritual, in its mater, manner and ends; and not at all civil: it essentially respects the inner man, and wholly labours (in the wayes appointed) the saving, edifying and perfecting of it. *Concl.* 8. This power is not properly *coercive*, *coactive*, and *compulsive*; but only *exclusive*: that is, if it be not obeyed by them, about whom it is exerced, it does debarre them from, and deny them the benefits, that are offered to all, and promised to the obedient. *Conel.* 9. This power, in the hands of the Church officers, is truly Chrifts, and when acted in his name, conforme to his lawes, is the exercife of his Supream dominion in and over the Church; By which he truly and visibly reigns over all in her: fo that obedience to this power, is obedience to Chrift, as King of his Church; and the contrare is high rebellion against him. *Concl.* 10. Al-

10. Although this power be only *Ministerial*, and *declarative* of the will of Christ; yet it is *authoritative*, and binding on all the Church, without exception of persons; and that on a double account, *first* on the account of divine commands enjoyning submission and obedience to its exercise, in the persons of those invested therewith; and also on the account of its respect to, and derivation from Christ, whose power and ordinance it is; and whom, in its exercise, it doeth represent to all. *Concl.* 11. This power is exercised, either singly & apart by every officer (according to the nature & measure of their power;) or in conjunction with one another, conforme to the precepts of the word, and practises of the Church in Scripture times. Although every officer of the Church in their several orders, have the whole power belonging *intrinsice* to it; yet there are some acts thereof, they cannot exerce, but in a conjunction with others, as ordaining of persons for the Ministry, Trying and censuring of scandalous and heretical Professours or Ministers, &c. for which there must be fixed meetings of officers, general and particular. *Concl.* 12. The ordinar officers of the Church (the extraordinare being ceased) are of three orders, Teachers and Pastors; Ruling elders, and Deacons. These we finde to be of divine institution, and no others: Many others have been brought into, and obtruded on the Church, but all of humane, or rather of diabolical invention; as, alace, their effects have sadly made out to the Church of God, in former and present times. In every one of these divine orders, we finde no institute superiority, in the same order, of one above others; as a Pastor of Pastors; or an Elder

of

of Elders; and a Deacon of Deacons: These who have assumed and exercised this superiority we cannot owne, as the Officers of Christ, nor subject to them, as such, till they prove their institution and mission from him; which yet they have not done. The outmost essey hath been for *Prelacy* or a *Bishop*, who is pleaded to be a Pastour of Pastours having the oversight of them and their flocks; but nothing attempted for making out the divine right of *Primats, Archbishops, Archpresbyters, Archdeacons,* &c.

This is that lowly and humble Government of the Church, that Christ hath institute in his word, and put in the hands of his Officers, commanding them to exercise and dispense the same to all in his house, under high paines: of which in the second place we assert these two. 1. That it is distinct and specifically different from the civil government of the Magistrat. And 2. That it is independant on it. These two conclusions we now undertake to prove, against the *Erastians* of our time, who assert, that when the Church comes to be embodyed with the Commonwealth, her Government becomes one with the Government of the State, and does not differ from it.

In opposition to these, we *affirme*, that when a Nation, State or Kingdom turnes Christian, in its Rulers and Subjects, the Government of the Church remaines specifically different and distinct from the Government of that State or Kingdome; as it was before its conversion to Christianity. The reasons perswading us of this, are 1. The Government of the Kingdome, that is not of this world, is distinct and different from the Government of the Kingdomes

domes that are of this world? But so it is, that the Government of the Church is the Government of a Kingdome, that is not of this world. Therefore the Government of the Church is distinct and different from the Government of the civil Magistrat, that is, the Government of Kingdomes that are of this world. This Argument leans on these three. 1. That the Church is a Kingdome, 2. That she hath a Government; And 3. That she is not of this world, although in it. All which are beyond disput clear from the Scriptures. All that our adversaries say to this, is, that the visible Church of Christ, is not properly, but metaphorically called a Kingdome: But how evident is the contrare? for is not Christ Jesus the Churches visible Head and King? Is she not ruled by his visible Lawes, Ordinances and Officers, that are properly and truely such? and are not all these from above, and not of this world?

Argum. 2. That Government whose supream Head, Lawes, Ordinances and Officers are specifically different from the Head, Lawes, Ordinances, and Officers of the civil Magistrat, must be distinct from it: But so it is that the head, lawes, ordinances and Officers of the Church are distinct from the lawes, &c. of the civil Magistrat: Therefore, &c. The reason of the *first proposition* is clear; for that which makes one Government differ from another, is different heads, lawes, Ordinances & Officers: where these are either numerically or specifically different, the Government is different accordingly: it being comprehended in all these: but that the supream head, laws, ordinances, and Officers of the Church are specifically different, from these of the civil Go-

vernment

vernment, who will deny it, that professes himself a Christian? *Obj.* But all these come under the inspection of the Magistrat, when he turns Christian. *Ans.* 1. Either these continue in the Church, under the Magistrats Government, what they were before; or they do not: if they do, the Argument holds, and proves the Government of the Church, to be distinct from that of the Magistrats, when Christian: If they do not continue, we ask from whence comes this alteration, and how will they prove it? Nothing here from our adversaries, but *Altum silentium*, or *nugæ*, destitute of all reason. But, 2. The tearm INSPECTION, or OVERSIGHT, is ambiguous; if by it we mean the countenancing, protecting, and encouraging of this Government of the Church, we yeeld it: but what sayes that to the confounding of the Governments; or making the Government of the Church, the Magistrats: if by inspection we understand, the devolving of the Government of the Church on the Magistrat, as the fountaine of it; the ordering and disposing of its exercise, the changing thereof at pleasure, in whole or in part: this we deny, and long have we looked for proofe; but have hitherto met with none.

Arg. 3. The Government of the Church formerly deliniated is incompatible with the civil Magistrats; therefore it is distinct from his Government. We hope, none will refuse this consequence. The *antecedent* is thus proven. (1.) The subordinat Government of the Church is purely *Ministerial*, not *dominative* or *imperial*; it is only *declarative*, and not *decisive*, not *coactive* and *compulsive*; it is exercised in Christs Name, and in his stead, and is the repre-
sentative

sentative of his special presence in his Church: these are incompatible with the Government of the Magistrat, whose power is Supream, Magisterial, and Imperial, coactive and compulsive; and exercised in his owne name, &c. (2.) The Magistrat cannot, yea may not exercise the Government of the Church, being disenabled thereto, by the commands and institutions of Christ, who hath laid the burden thereof on others, and not on him. The most grant, the Magistrat himself may not exercise some parts of this Government, as ordaining of persons for the Ministery, excommunicating, &c. and why he may do other parts and acts belonging to it, and not these, We desire proofe: all our antagonists arguments in this conclude for the whole. *Obj.* But some Magistrats have exercised both powers, as *Moses, Samuel, David, Solomon*, &c. *Ans.* These were both Magistrats and Prophets; and it is evident from the Scripture, that what they did either in constituting or in exercising of the Government of the Church, they did it as Prophets, and not as Magistrats: we find Magistrats, that were not Prophets, attempting it, & reprehended for so doing, as *Saul, Uzziah*: which says, that it did not belong to their Magistratical Office.

Arg. 4. That Goverment that is founded upon and regulated by another rule and instrument, then the law of the civil Magistrat, is distinct from his Goverment: But the Government of the Church is founded upon, and ruled by another law or rule, then the Magistrats; the law and word of Christ: therefore, &c. the *first proposition* is clear, for the Government of the Magistrat does flow from and is regulated

lated by his owne lawes, of which he is the sole fountaine: The *second*, we suppose, is undenyable among Christians, who acknowledge the Scriptures for a rule of Doctrine, Worship and Government to the Church of Christ. *Obj.* But there are somethings necessare to the Government of the Church, not contained in the Scriptures ? *Ans.* This we deny. For 1. What the Scriptures containe, anent the Government of the Church (if reduced to practice) is able to attaine its ends, and more is not necessary: Let the Church have these, and the work will be done: we make & feigne necessities, but no more is necessar to the ends of the Church Government, then what is determined by the Scriptures anent it. (2.) The ability of the Churches Government, for reaching its ends, lyes not in the innate sufficiency of its instituted means ; but in the Spirit of Christ, working with, in, and by them ; by which low, weak and despicable wayes, Christ carries on the salvation of his people, that the excellency of the power may be of him, and not of us. (3.) The Scriptures being a full and perfect rule for all maters of faith and obedience, what it containes of, and anent the Government of the Church, must be perfect and sufficient: sure we are, the Churches Government is a good work, and its exercise, acts of obedience to Christ Jesus ; anent which it is said 1. *Tim.* 3. The Scripturs are able to make the Man of God perfect, throughly furnished to every good work. (4.) We enquire, when the Church is without a Christian Magistrat, and under the feet of a heathenish persecuting one (in which case our opposits grant her a Government distinct from, and independent on the Magistrat) whether the

the Government exercised in her, be able to attaine its ends. If it be (as the experience of the Church in this case puts beyond doubt) why may it not do the same, under a Christian Magistrat?

Arg. 5. That Goverement that is exercised in the name of another distinct Supream Head, besides the Magistrat, is distinct from the Government of the civil Magistrat. But the Government of the Church is exerced in the name and authority of another Supream head, not subordinat to the Magistrat. Therefore, &c. What can be said to the *first proposition*, we understand not; for all Governments one with, and subordinat to the Magistrat, are exercised in his name and authority: But this Government of the Church is exercised in her, in the name of Christ Jesus, by his Officers, as is clear from the word.

Arg. 6. The designations, denominations and relations, in and with which the Church is represented in the Scriptures, do also confirme this truth; she is called the *Body of Christ*, the *Kingdome of Heaven*, the *City of God*, the *House of the living God*, *the new Jerusalem*. As all these do necessarily import a Government in the Church; so they insinuat the same to be different from all other Governments: Which we may mould into this Argument. That society which is the body of Christ, &c. must have a Government distinct from the Government of the civil Magistrat: But the Church is that society, that is only the body of Christ, &c. Therefore, &c. *Obj.* But all these are said only of the invisible Church? *Ans.* But the contrare is clear from those Scriptures, where these Epithets are given to the Church, 1 Cor: 12. 1 Tim. 3. 15.

K *Arg.* 7.

Arg. 7. That Government whose immediat and essential ends are specifically different, from the immediat and essential ends of the Magistrats Government, is distinct from the Government of the Magistrat: But here it is so: the essential & immediat ends of Church Government, are different from the essential & immediat end of Magistracy; as will be clear to any that compares them together; The ends of Church Government are the saveing of the soule, the conversion and edification of sinners, &c. The ends of Magistracy, are, the outward publick peace and prosperity of the common wealth, the execution of justice in the maintaining and preserving of propriety, &c. with these the Churches government does not medle, nor intend them, of it self. *Obj.* The Magistrat ought to intend, and endeavour the spiritual happinesse and wellfare of his subjects? *Ans.* We grant this, but as all others ought to do it; for every one in their station are bound to designe and labour the eternal salvation of these under their charge; this being a common end, that all Christians, in their several capacities, should seek after, in their love to one another: the *first proposition* is evident, because the specificall distinction betwixt powers, habits and acts, is taken from their Objects and immedia proper ends; Where these diff·r, they are by al Philosophers constitute into different species's.

In the next place *we assert.* That as the government of the Church does specifically differ from the government of the Magistrat; so it is independan thereon, and not directly subordinat thereto. A truth (how much soever it be decryed) we are not shamed of, nor affrayed to profess & maintaine; and

whose

I lay aside prejudice and earthly inter-
der these reasons with us, will be forc-
dge it.
e Magistrat is not the fountaine of
; it hath not its derivation from him;
s not directly subordinat to him: The
founded on this truth, granted by all
ivines, that all power directly subordi-
pendant on the Magistrat, is derived
e fountaine thereof: the *antecedent* we
(1.) The Magistrat as a Magistrat is
of the Church, but as a Professor of
which intitles others to this priviledge,
n; Therefore he cannot be the foun-
h power as such; for whoever is the
wer to any society, is a member, yea
ember of it; *Obj.* But as a christian
is a member of the Church? *Ans* 1.
ill this prove him to be the fountaine
wer? so might Christian Husbands,
. argue as justly for this clame: the
being only a member of the Church,
and not as a Magistrat, Magistracy
nore priviledge, then any other power,
al, when the person turnes Christian;
e of membership goes on grounds and
oon to all Christians; and containes no
ne more then to another. If any think
loes, they shall do well to prove it,
ath yet offered to do. 2. If men un-
, what it is to be a Christian, a disci-
ber of Christ's Church, they would
i inconsistency with the said profession;
K 2   does

does not perfons, turning Chriftians, profeffe fubje[ction]
[c]tion to Chrift, his Lawes, Ordinances and Servant[s]
which is repugnant to the fountaine of the Churc[h]
power. (2.) He may not exercife Church powe[r]
Therefore is not the fountaine of it: all yeeld, th[at]
thefe who are the fountaine of power to others m[ay]
exercife it themfelves, it being in them, and othe[rs]
acting, as their delegates, in its exercife: that t[he]
Magiftrat may not exercife Church power, is clea[r]
for Church power, being by pofitive inftitutio[n]
from Chrift, they that exercife it muft have a co[m]
miffion from him, which none hath produced f[or]
the Magiftrat: *Eraftus* afferteth it, but without [a]
proofe, of which it is fo deftitute, that the moft [of]
his followers have left him in this affertion.

Arg. 2. All Church power is lodged in and i[m]
mediatly defcended from Chrift Jefus, as the S[u]
pream Head and Ruler of the Church, and Superio[r]
to the Magiftrat: Therefore it is not fubordinat [to]
the Magiftrat: The reafon of the confequence is cle[ar]
for it is a repugnancy in a power to be immediat[ly]
fubordinat to two Supream powers, in one and t[he]
fame refpects; efpecially where the one is fuperio[r]
to the other: The *antecedent* is manifeft, for Chr[ift]
is only head of the Church; all power in her is inf[ti]
tute by him; exerced in his name; aftricted to, a[nd]
regulated by his word; and accomptable to him. A[ll]
notes of power immediatly defcended from hi[m]
Obj. But the Chriftian Magiftrat, as Chrifts fubf[ti]
tute and vicegerent, is under him, the neareft and i[m]
mediat fountaine of Church power; for *fubordina[ta]
non pugnant? Anf.* Long hath the *Pope of Rome* co[n]
tended for this, and on grounds more plaufible, th[an]

these, on which the Magistrat goes. But Protestant Divines answer to the Papists on this head, furnish us with irrefragable answers to the Magistrats clame; which we desire our adversaries would consider & answer at their own leasure: we finde not the Magistrat inrolled among the officers of the Church, far lesse substitute for Chrifts vicegerent; if there be any Scripture for this, bring it forth? We know of none as yet alledged by our adversaries; but what will plead as strongly, for the heathenish Magistrat, as for the Christian: And if they do, what traitours were the Apostles, Ministers and Christians of the primitive times, that did not acknowledge the heathenish Magistrates for their head in the Church; but resisted and disobeyed their lawes and edicts against them, for setting up of another King, in the maters of their Christian Profession.

Arg. 3. All Church power was institute by Christ, in an immediat subordination to himself; without any acknowledgment of, or dependance on the Magistrat: Therefore it is not dependant upon, nor subordinat to him: The *antecedent* is clear from the History of the New Testament, where we find, that Christ moulded and constituted the Church by his Apostles, and furnished her with a Government and officers, to be exercised in his name; and all this he did without consulting, or advising with the Magistrat, or suspending of her upon him; the Magistrat all this time resisting & setting himself, for crushing of his Church & Kingdome of Christ; which he erected in the midst of their Kingdomes, making use of their rage and violence to establish and propagat it, for some Hundreds of years. All this is so evident, that

K 3 our

our adversaries are not able to refuse it; what is the[re]
then to hinder the consequence, that we draw from t[he]
deed of Christ? If our opposites in this mater cou[ld]
shew us, that the Church had no government institu[te]
by Christ; nor exercised any, all the time that the M[a-]
gistrat thus opposed himself to her; or that Christ h[ad]
declared his will, that she should be subjected to t[he]
Magistrat in her Government, when he should b[e-]
come Christian; they would soon end this strife: b[ut]
nothing can we learne from them to this purpose.

Arg. 4. As this Government was institute [by]
Christ and his Apostles; so it was exerced in his nar[ne]
in the Church, without dependance on the Mag[i-]
strat, till *Constantine* the great's time; and fro[m]
thence downeward, till the Reformation of Reli[gi-]
on brack up in *Germanie*: till which time, it w[as]
never questioned by any, until *Erastus* the Physici[an]
arose, who laboured not only to subject the Chur[ch]
to the Magistrat, in all her concearnes as such; b[ut]
denied all Government to her by divine institutio[n,]
that is distinct from the Government of the Ma[gi-]
strat; contrare to full and clear Scripture, whic[h]
he most insolently and wickedly endeavours to wre[st]
& pervert. So then if the Government of the Churc[h]
was in Scripture times, and downwards, till withi[n]
these hundered years, exercised without dependan[ce]
on the Magistrat, both heathenish and Christian[,]
then it must yet be independant on, and not directl[y]
subordinat to him. Here our Antagonists are put t[o]
strange shifts: The first three hundred years, the[y]
must grant; and may we not take this for a yeeldin[g]
of the cause? Scripture and antiquity hath been hel[d]
for a sufficient plea, for maters of doctrine and pra[-]
ctic[e]

tife: debates in Polemical divinity hath run on these two heads; and whoever made out their assertions from these, have been esteemed to carry the cause: all that our adversaries have to say to this, are these two. 1. That the Government exercised in the Church was not by divine institution and precepts; but by confederation of Churches and officers. To this we reply. 1. If the Epistles to *Timothy*, to the seven Churches in *Asia*. *Revel*. 2. and 3. *Chapters*; with other places of Scripture, used by our Divines, in this mater, prove not the contrary, they have no sense: We beg of our adversaries, they will, for saving us a labour, answer Mr. *Gillespies* Arguments from Scripture, in the second part of his *Aarons Rod blossoming*. 2. Besids they are not able to make out what they assert, to wit, that the Church did exercise her Government in these times, by confederation and mutual consent; and not by institution and command: or as there is nothing in Scripture and pure antiquity for this; So the Churches being gathered and constitute by the Apostles, we presume, they continued in the constitutions, which the Apostles left, according to the precepts and rules they gave them; to which we find, in the word and Church History, their practice conforme. When the persecutions of the Church ceased, upon the Magistrats turning Christian, we find her continuing, in the exercise of the former Government, (but with the addition of some corruptions, which grew to a sad hight afterwards, throw the excessive munificence & bounty of *Constantine* the Great, the first Christian Emperour) and exercising the same, as formerly; as is clear from History; that speaks of these times. Here our adversaries speak of some instances of the power, the Magistrat did exerce in the Church; as convocating of Synods, labouring in the peace of the Church, sorely rent at some times, through sad heresies and schisms; And that saying of *Constantines* repeated by them, *ad nauseam: vos estis Episcopi ad intra, Ego ad extra*. But how is our Antagonists conclusion made out by all these? will it follow, that becaus the Magistrat did convocat Synods, its Government is derived from, & subordinat to him? No wayes, for (1.) Albeit the Magistrat have a power to convocat the officers of the Church, anent maters relating to his owne conscience and duty, whether about Church or State; yet this is not privative of the Churches power to convocat her owne assemblies, either for worship or government; as we find she did in the primitive times, not only without but against his consent; yea when the Magistrat became Christian, she retained and exercised this power in assembling into several Synods, without the Magistrat. It is true, we do not read of general Synods assembled, after this, but by the Magistrat, till the *Pope* of *Rome*, claimed this power, and usurped therein on the Church and Magistrat, as he did in all other things, but the vastness of the Empire, and large extent of the Church (which exceeded its bounds) made this in point of prudence necessare, for without the Magistrat, it could not easily be done. But (2.) Convocating of others, is not alwayes, in its self, an infallible signe of a superiour power and dominion over judicatories convocated; as in limited Monarchies, and not absolute, where the Supream power is lodged in the King and States of the Kingdom; although the

King

King have the power of couveening the States; yet they share with him, in the legiſlative and executive power, while in being: therefore the illation is bad and not concludent (4.) What imaginable advantage can accrew, to our adverſaries aſſertion, by that ſaying of *Conſtantines*, formerly cited? We grant, the Magiſtrat is the overſeer of things without the Church; but this will not prove, that the government of the Church, is in and from his hands, and ſubordinat to him; they muſt firſt make it appear by good reaſon, that her Government is *ad extra*, which they have not yet done, nor never will; for although it be viſible in its inſtitution and exerciſe; yet it is as intrinſinck to, and within her, as her doctrine and worſhip; which by this fence, will be as much derived from and ſubjected to the Magiſtrat, as her Government; ſeing the one is as viſible in its diſpenſation, as the other.

Arg. 5. The Magiſtrat may not, yea cannot *jure* impede and hinder the exerciſe of the Churches government: therefore it is not derived from, nor ſubjected to him: the reaſon of this conſequence is, whatever power is derived from the Magiſtrat, and ſubordinated directly to him, he may ſuſpend, hinder its exerciſe, yea he may totally remove and annihilat it: this is yeelded by all, and taken for a ſure Maxime in Politicks: but the Magiſtrat may not do this, in the Government of the Church; and that becauſe it is of divine inſtitution, and the perſons intruſted with, and called to its exerciſe, are under the obligations of divine precepts and commands for it, which the Magiſtrat cannot hinder, nor by any deed or command of his, make void. Theſe that deny

this

this divine institution of Church Government, we refer to the forecited book; where it is strongly pleaded & made out from clear and express Scriptures in the New Testament. Likewise as he cannot impede its exercise, so he may not nullity its sentences, by himself, which he may do in the sentences passed by all powers, derived from and subordinat to himself.

Arg. 6. The Christian Magistrat, is by vertue of his Christian Profession, bound to subject himself to the acts & exercise of Church Government, in the hand of Church Officers; and is as much obleidged to yeeld thereto, as any other: Therefore Church power is not directly subordinat to him. The antecedent is clear; for all are commanded submission and obedience to Church Officers, in the exercise of their power, in watching, overseeing, and ruleing of the Church *Heb.* 13. 7, 17. to which exercise of their power, we finde Magistrats in the word submitting, as *UZZIA*, who was by the priests, conforme to the law, separated and secluded from the holy things of God, and communion with the Church in these; yea, it is given for the maine cause of all that heavy wrath and judgment, that came on *Zedekiah* 2. *Chron.* 36. 12. that he humbled not himself before *Jeremiah*, the Prophet, speaking the word of the Lord to him. *Obj.* But this subjection in Magistrats to Church Officers, is properly to Christ, and not to them? *Ans.* we confess, the subjection is primarily and cheifly to Christ Jesus, whom such, in the exercise of their Office, doe represent; yet the subjection is to them too, whom all, without exception of any in the Church, are commanded to receive, hear and obey: so that in the dispensation of holy things, they are
superiour

superiour to all in the Church, Magistrats and others, as their constitut Rulers, Overseers, Governours and Watch men, whom they ought to obey; when acting in their Office, agreeable to the law of Christ: which obedience is not *CATACHRESTICAL* or *ABUSIVE* (as *VIDELIUS* speaks) in the Magistrat, but proper and really, a debt they owe to the Ministers of the Gospel dispensing holy things, as much as any other member of the Church; their obligation to it being of the same kinde and nature, with the obligation of others. If any think otherwayes, let them produce their reasons and Scriptures.

2. If the fiery and zealous promotters of the Magistrats power, in and over the Church of God, did consider the true and real prejudice they do to Magistrats, by exeeming them from that subjection, that they, with all others, owe to Church Officers, they would (if there be any sense of Religion and its advantages remaining with men) hold their hand; and should have little thanks from Magistrats, for their preposterous zeal, who, by their opinions in this mater, do really exclude Magistrats from the Communion of the Church, and the benefite of the ordinance of Church Government, which in its designe and effects is for saving of the soul, as well as all other ordinances. Other Arguments might be adduced, as the want of power in the Magistrat to alter and change the Government of the Church; or to nullify its just sentences passed, &c.

SECT.

Sect. VII.

The sinfulness of the Ecclesiastick Supreamacy manifested.

BUt judging these sufficient to the conviction of the unprejudged; we come to the other part of our task, which is to shew, that this visible intrinsick government of the Church is assumed by, and given to our Rulers, in the present standing laws of the Kingdom; which we shall make out from the *acts of Parliament*; particularly *act of restitution. Parl.* 1. Sess. 2. *Act.* 1. *act anent the National Synod Parl.* 1. Sess. 3. *Act.* 4. *act against Conventicles Parl.* 2. Sess. 5. *act against Keepers of Conventicles and withdrawers &c. Parl.* 2. Sess. 3. *Act.* 17. *act against unlawful ordinations Parl.* 2. Sess. 3. with others of the like nature. But before we enter on the probation of this, it will be necessare, for clearing our way to it, to consider a little two things, in the beginning of the narrative of the act of restitution, repeated in several acts: where, *first*, the Government of the Church is called the external Government of the same: the tearm, EXTERNAL, being Notourly ambiguous, should have been explained, & all not left to guess at its meaning: EXTERNAL is by some opposed to the *internal invisible Government of Christ* on the souls of his people; and so by it they understand, the visible intrinsick Government of the visible Church: that this is meant by the tearm EXTERNAL GOVERNMENT, in this and other acts, the following Arguments undertake to make out: but
some

some others oppose the terme *EXTERNAL GOVERNMENT*, to this intrinsick visible Government of the Church, formerly described and asserted to be distinct from, and independant on the Magistrat; and by it they do understand, these humane adjuncts and accidents, that are civil in themselves, and not made sacred by divine institution: some plead this to be the sense of these terms, in the acts of Parlt; but how groundlesly let our subsequent reasons determine. *Secondly*, It is there said, that the ordering and disposing of the external government of the Church belongs to the Crowne, &c. it is hard to sense this; for ordering and disposing, when done by persons in authority, is a part of government in it self; and if it be so, the Phrase is equivalent to this, the governing of the external government of the Church: which is a strange sort of speach, as if a government needed a government to governe it: What if this were said of the government of the government of the State? Would it not be reputed non-sense? But the truth is, all governments do necessarily imply a power to dispose and order all things relating to it, as a part of the same; & without which it were imperfect; and it is without disput evident from the experience of the Church under heathenish Magistrats; that the government of the Church had this, which by this act is taken from her. *Next*, we ask, whether this ordering and diposing be an act of the Ecclesiastick or civil government? If it be of the Ecclesiastick, it is againe non-sense, at the best; and is as much as if it had been said, the Ecclesiastical governing of the Ecclesiastical government of the Church; a perfect tautology, But if it be an be an act of the civil government; how comes it, that in this and other act of Parliament, it is called the *Kings Ecclesiastical Government*, in opposition to the civil? *Obj.* It is only objectively so called. *Ans.* Then it is properly and formally civil, the phrase, objectively Ecclesiastical being *CATACHRE-STICAL* and *ABUSIVE*; a very improper speach; yea as improper, as if we should call Church power or Government, in the hands of Church officers, objectively civil, or civil. *Thirdly*, In the last place we desire to know, whether this ordering or disposing of the Government of the Church be necessary, or not? If it be not necessary, why is the Church troubled with it? If it be, we ask againe, when it was exercised by the Church, whether it was an act of civil or Church Government? It could not be of the civil; for the Church had none under persecuting Magistrats; if it was an act of the Ecclesiastical or Church Government; then it was purely and formally such; and not truely civil, although exercised about things civil in their owne nature, and seing it was so, how comes it to be the Magistrats now? To any considerat and unbyassed reader, it will be manifest, that these words or expressions come from mindes, designing the enhansing of the intrinsick visible Government of the Church, and withall labouring to cover it; but all in vaine.

Now that the Ecclesiastical Government of the Church, formally and intrinsically such, is assumed by, and given to the Magistrat, in the present standing lawes, will be apparent to any that consider these things, in the forecited *acts* of *Parliament*. (1.) That Church officers, in the exercise of Church go-

vernment

heir Church assemblies or judicatories,
adance upon, and subordinated to the
eam to them therein: this makes the
aine of Church power, & the Church
ve and hold their power of him; which
g the proper Head of the Church, &
in Chrifts roome to her. (2.) The go-
e Church, thus subjected to & depen-
ig as Supream, is, in the *act of restitution*,
id made to take in ordination, acts of
licting of Church censures; yea to all
atters formally Ecclesiastical; to all,
Church power is exerced, he is made
(3.) All Church power and jurisdi-
vas exercised in this Church (before
luction of prelacy) without this deri-
ind subordination to the Magistrat, is
annulled; certainly in these times, the
l and did exercise a power about Church
is to be seen in the laws then made in
; but this does not now content, with-
emacy; which imports another power
the Magistrat now, that was not then.
remacy, and (as it is called) the *Royal*
the Crown, is given for the maine rea-
hange made in the Government of the
overturning and casting out of the true
, that then was, and bringing in ano-
ad, without the authority and concur-
Church: a fair opened doore, for bring-
e alteration and change in doctrine and
hen there is access to it. (5.) Prelacy by
estored, not only to the former height
it was

it was at, and had attained by law and practice, before its last ejection out of this Church: but also to all that ever it was, even in the times of popery; which, when considered, in the constitution and priviledges it then had, was an humane Office founded on the Supremacy of the *Pope*; but now, by this law, on the Magistrat: which sayes, that although the persons be changed, yet the Supremacy is the same. (6.) In the act anent the *National Synod*, the nomination and election of persons, by whom the government of the Church is to be exercised, under the King, is asserted to be the Kings, by vertue of his royal prerogative and supremacy, in causes Ecclesiastical; so that the constitution of Church judicatories is made dependant upon him: a thing never heard of nor practised in this or any other Church, till of late. (7.) The right, being and constitution of the National Synod of this Church, is wholly dependant upon, and derived from this law; So as it is no Synod of this Church, that is not gathered, and constitute conforme to it; although a Synod in this Church should have all, that made Synods lawful, and their acts obligatory, in former times. (8.) The particular constitution of this National Synod, as to its members, (which in this act are nominated, and regulated thereby, for all future times) is determined for its times and places of meeting, and put wholly in the Kings hand, and asserted to be his right, by vertue of his Supremacy over this Church: It is no Synod that is not thus convocated. (9.) The maters to be handled, debated, and concluded in this Synod (a thing alwayes judged intrinsick to the Church) comes only from the King, & are to be proposed

posed from him, by the *Arch-prelat of Saint Andrews* and no other: a fearful restraining of the divine liberty of the Ministers of the Gospel, who may not speak of maters of doctrine & manners, (although necessary for the times) contrare to the freedome, that is commanded them by their master, anent these. (10.) The King's, or his Commissioners presence is made essential to the constitution, and of binding force to this nationall Synod: It is no Synod, although constitute after the paterne of Church Synods, in the primitive times; if it want this. (11.) No mater debated and concluded by the Majority of this Synod, is obligatory on this Church, and its members, if not approven and allowed by the King or his Commissioner. This suspends the intrinsick obligation of Synods on the King; so that no canon, act or constitution, do binde the members of the Church, if he assent not: As this secures the Court in their carnal liberties and sinful wayes; so it shuts the door on all endeavours of reformation by the Church, when Princes are vicious. (12.) In the act asserting the Kings Supremacy Ecclesiastick, the King & his successors are enabled and impowered to medle with all maters and meetings Ecclesiastick, which brings the doctrine and worship within his verge, and subjects the same to him, as much as the government. (13.) They are impowered to enact and emit constitutions, acts, and orders, anent maters and meetings Ecclesiastick, as they please and think fit, and are not, in the making of these, astricted to any rule, but their pleasure, O HORRENDUM! (14.) All these acts and orders they may statute, independant on the Church, Parliament, or any other, by their sole authority

L

thority, never granted to any of his predecessours before. (15.) These acts and constitutions insert, the book of Councel, and duely published, are declared and made to be of full force and obligation to this Church and her members. No need of Synod here, which by this are wholly subverted. (16.) All former lawes, acts and clauses of them, contrare to and inconsistent with this, are made void, cassed annulled; which takes away the Protestant Religion the Word of God as the rule, the concurrence of the Church in the assistance of the constitutions Ecclesiastical, that was provided and secured by former acts of Parliament: a wide door for Popery. (17.) In the act against unlawful Ordinations (as they call them) the Ordination of persons to the Ministry, by Ministers of Christ Jesus, that have not conformed to Prelacy, (which was held unquestionable & valid for its substance by all, till this late gang of Prelats arose, in which they are degenerat from their predecessours) is, by the sole authority of the Magistrat made void; and all Ministerial acts, and Church benefites depending thereon, declared to be nul. An act that unchristians and condemns all the reformed Churches, making their Churches no Ministerial political Churches, and all Ordinances, dispensed in them, nullities: which their practice at this time in *England* does confirme; while Romish Priests turning Protestants, are, without ordination, made capable, and advanced to Church places and preferments; of which the Protestant Ministers of other Churches, conforming to Prelacy, are denied, till they be reordained. Other mediums contained in other acts of Parliaments, for fixing of the preceeding

conclusi-

(163)

ve paſſe; having hinted at ſome of them
ng theſe ſufficient, for the conviction
ſſed & unprejudged; who through the
and earthly intereſt, have not caſt
of the word, but keeps in ſubjection

the laſt place anſwer ſome objections;
have to do with two ſortes of per-
ne high flowne *Eraſtians* of our times,
it of no government in the Church, but
n and from the Magiſtrat whoſe de-
is evident from the act aſſerting the
acy) is, to take all Government out of
hands; and to put it on the King & his
be only exerciſed by them: which,
like of Prelacy, is not ſufficiently la-
to heart, nor reſiſted by many, as its
ſequences, to all the concerns of the
equire. Beſides theſe, there are who,
rinciple is not yet known,) think that
y, as it is now aſſerted by law, is not
leſiaſtical, but only objectively ſo;
ge: ſome of the objections. of the firſt
e met with, as we went along the for-
ve know of no other, beſides theſe, of
ole ſtrength, but one.
the Magiſtrat being the keeper of both
aw; of the table of Religion, as well
: of Righteouſneſs; ought to have a care
and hath power given him to exerciſe
me? *Anſwer*, This being the *Achilles*
ns, and *ſemi Eraſtians*; of *VIDELIUS*
We ſhall returne theſe anſwers to it;

L 2 and

and shew it cannot bear their conclusion. 1. What ever power the Christian Magistrat can clame by this, the heathenish Magistrat hath the same; he is by his Magistratical office constitute, *in actu primo*, a Keeper of both tables; as is evident from, Rom. 13: 1, 2. If he do not exercise it, it comes not from any defect of power in his office, or the institution of it; but from his blindness and unbeleef, which indisposes him to answer his trust, and to do the work of his office; to which, upon the revelation of the Gospel he is bound: and seing it is so, either the Church, in exercising of her Government independantly of heathenish Magistrats, usurped on his office & power; which the adversary dare no say: Or els the Christian Magistrat hath no more power in & over the Church, then the other had: and therefore the Church, in exercising her power under the Christian Magistrat, does not usurp upon him, more then on the other. 2. The Ministers of the Gospel are by vertue of their office, Keepers of both tables of the law, of the table of Righteousness, as well as of the table of Religion: will it from thence follow that they may medle with the Magistrats office, and assume its exercise; or that the same does depend on them? No wayes: and yet the consequence is as good in the one as in the other: by the same medium we shall prove Ministers, have as good right and power to manage the affairs of the State; as the Magistrat hath (in our adversaries sense) to manage the affairs of the Church. We know they will reject the consequence with disdaine, as to Ministers, and ask for our proofe, for which, we grant, they have just cause so we deny the consequence as to the Magistrat, to

which

which they have not given us yet any colourable proofe; but dictator-like assert it. The truth is, every man in his capacity is a Keeper of both tables of the law; but in doing of it, is to hold within the compasse of his station, the nature, and limites of the power granted him; and is not to invade the office and power of others, nor the work proper thereto: as is evident from multitude of precepts in the Word of God. So if Ministers, notwithstanding their being Keepers of the tables of the law, may not invade the Magistrats office and power; So neither may Magistrats invade the Ministerial office and power. 3. The acts and wayes of the Magistrats keeping of the tables of the law, should answer, and be agreable to the nature, extent, and limits of his office & power; within the verge of which, he is to walk, as all others are to do in theirs: As Ministers are to keep both the tables of the law by preaching the word, dispensing of Ordinances, and exercising of discipline, according to the rules of the word; to which they are impowered by the institutions and commands of Christ, without dependance on the Magistrat; so the Magistrat is to keep them likwise, by commanding all to their several duties, protecting them therein by the sword, which is given him for that end; executing of justice in punishing of evil doers, and rewarding the good, &c. but is not to medle with the Government of the Church, in whole or in part; but to see that it be done by these, whom Christ hath called to and intrusted with it.

It is *objected* by others, that it is not the intrinsick visible and internal Government of the Church, that the Magistrat assumes, in the acts of Parliament; it is is only the external Government, that is expressly so called, in the act of restitution? *Anf.* This is materially Answered above; but that we may be distinct, there are two things belonging to the Church. (1.) The outward and external adjuncts or accidents; As the *Biotica* or *Mundana*, Stipends Manse Glybs, outward liberty and peace, &c. (2.) The proper and true objects of Church Government or power, that are intrinsick to it, although visible; as the Word, Ordinances, Ministery and necessary circumstances &c. It is not the *first* of these but the *second* that the act of restitution with other acts do truely mean, as is undoubtedly made out by the former arguments; as particularly the first three that it is the Church judicatories; the maters handled in and by them, proper thereto, that constitute the King Supream; these being essential and intrinsick to the Government of the Church, in its several parts: he that is made supream to these, is made supream to the Church, and all that appertaine to her.

Obj. 2. But it is only the ordering and disposeing of the Government, that is declared to belong to the King. *Anf.* It is so said in that act, but it is evident from the mater and frame of it, that it is the Government in whole that is truely meant and intended, as is formerly proven. But 2. Ordering and disposing of things, proper and specifick to any Government, is a part of the Government it self; and to whom the Government belongs, the ordering of it belongs likewise: by the same reasons that any shall undertake to prove, that the ordering and disposeing of the civil Government belongs to the Magistrat

giſtrat; we shall prove the ordering and diſpoſing of the Church's Government does belong to Church Officers: no Government can be perfect without it, or able to attaine its ends, and therefore muſt neceſſarily be implyed in, and intrinſick to it.

Obj. 3. But there are ſome acts of Church power the Magiſtrat may do, as convocating of Synods, determining of circumſtances, indicting of publick faſts and thankſgivings? *Anſ.* As we deny all formal Church power to the Magiſtrat, and all acts formally proceeding therefrom; ſo we grant there are acts, *Firſt*, ſome common as prayer, rebuking, inſtructing of others, and others of the like nature: which, when they come from a Church Officer, are *authoritative* and acts of Church power; that are yet performable by others, in their ſtations, and (ſo to ſpeak) are *charitative*. 2. Some are proper and only belongs to Church Officers, as preaching of the Goſpel, diſpenſing of the Sacraments, exerciſe of Church diſcipline, &c. We doe not deny, but chierfully grant (wiſhing with all our hearts, there were many ſuch Magiſtrats in the Church) that the Magiſtrat ought to rebuke, to exhort, admoniſh, inſtruct & pray, &c. As all others in their ſtations and offices ſhould do; but from thence it will not follow, that he may exerciſe formal acts of Church power, more then others; or that the Church power is dependant on him: the Conſequence is wide. But to the particular inſtances; as, that of convocating of Synods or any Church judicatory, we ſay, it is within the verge of his power, as a Magiſtrat, who may and ought to command all within his dominions, to their ſeveral duties, and Miniſters among others, as they

ought

ought to doe to him, so the Magistrats convocating of Ministers, is but a putting of them to their duty, which in the Magistrat is no act of Church power; but an act of his office he owes to all. 2. This act or deed of the Magistrat, is not privative of the same in the Officers of the Church, who may & ought come together of themselves, as the necessities of the Church requires. On the by, it is an evil consequence; the Magistrat may gather Synods; therefore Ministers may not doe it: It is like to this, others may rebuke, admonish, &c. Therefore Ministers may not doe it. For although the Magistrat have an imperative power, over all; yet it is not privative of any power in others, that is proper to their station and office. (2.) As for the determining of the circumstances in Government, we reply, there are two sorts of circumstances relateing to these, first some extrinsick, and not in themselves simply necessare, although convenient; as Churches of such and such formes, pulpets, ornaments, &c. These, being in their natural use civil, belong to the Magistrat, and are directly under his power, to order and dispose. *Next* 2. There are some circumstances intrinsick to the actions of worship and Government, and so connected therewith, in that degree of necessity, that they cannot be performed without them; and come within the compass of divine commands, on which, the morality of individual actions, as to their goodnes and evil, *pro hic & nunc* does depend; as such and such persons, doctrines, times, places, helps, &c. which all moralists and divines make to specify all humane actions, as to their morality *in individuo*. Of these we assert, that the determination of them,

as

:ct worship and Government, and are
th them, belongs to the Officers of the
l not to the Magiſtrat: we have given
for this before, as 1. we ſee commands
Church about them, and not to the
1. Cor. 14. 2. If the determination
in the Magiſtrats power, it should be
power, to hinder, impede and obſtruct
hip and Government, in its exerciſe, at
for whoever hath theſe things in his
out which, the actions of worship and
cannot be performed, hath the actions
to hinder or not. 3. The conſequen-
g this to the Magiſtrat are miſcheivous:
if he do not wholly hinder the exerciſe
:rial office and power; yet he may re-
it it ſo, as to bring them under dread-
neſs in their Miniſtry or office; he may
ip from preaching ſuch and ſuch do-
, at ſuch and ſuch times and in ſuch
calleth them to preach. As for the
:e, for indicting of dayes for ſolemne
umiliation or of thankſgiving; we ſay,
on it among theſe common duties of
t every Chriſtian, in his ſtation, is bound
and of God to obſerve; and according
of their power to ſee them obſerved by
hem, when the diſpenſations of mercy
t cals them to theſe; as is clear from
and examples we have in the word; ſo
tians, in their ſeveral capacities, offices,
extent of the ſame, have the power of
keeping of ſuch times and dayes; as

L 5 Maſters

Masters in families, pastours in congregations, or in their associations, and Magistrats, &c. From this it will not follow, that Magistrats, Masters of Families, &c. their indicting of such dayes for divine exercises, is an act of Church power; although it be such in the Officers of the Church, and as it comes from them: no more then others rebuking, exhorting, &c. is an act of Church authority and power, although it be so from them. 2. That it only belongs to the Magistrat to indict dayes of publict fastings, or of thanksgiving, & not to the pastours of the Church, where hath our antagonists learned this? We grant the Magistrat participats with others in this power; but the nature of these duties, the precepts, and examples of the word, impowers others in their capacities, as much as him: it were easy to make this out. We acknowledge, for the more harmony in this publict work, and convenient following of it with benefite and advantage to Church and State, it were expedient, that Magistrats and Ministers did previously consult, and agree about publict fasts and thanksgiving: but to affirme this, to the privation of the power and obligations, laid on others anent it, is not only an encroachment on the divine rights of others, but a loosing of these bonds, with which God hath tyed them; and what is this but to fight against God in the persones of his Creaturs.

Obj. 4. Seing Ministers are bound to give an accompt to the Magistrat, when required, of what they do, in the Government of the Church; will it not follow, they are subordinat to him in so far, in its exercise? *Ans.* No wayes; for (1.) They stand oblidged to do the like to all others, over whom the they are set, and do rule; when their carriage in the Ministry is stumbling and offensive to them; to which they are oblidged, both by general and particular precepts; and yet it will not follow, that in their Ministry they are subordinat to such. (2.) The Magistrat, by vertue of his professed subjection to Christ, is bound to give an accompt of his actings in his Government to Ministers and others, when he proveth scandalous and offensive: which many of them have done. To this they are oblidged, both on the accompt of their promised subjection to the word, its ordinances, and Christs servants, dispensing the same; and likewise on the accompt of Charity and love, that binds all, not only to endeavour the preventing, but removing of offences, when given; to which the Magistrat is as incident, in his capacity, as others; as alas sad experience puts beyond debate!

Obj. 5. But as the Government of the Church, and its exercise, is the object of the Magistrats power and its acts; does he not act about those imperially, and *Architectonice*? And if it be so, is he not Supream to & above the Ministers of the Church, and they subordinat to him? *Ans.* This is the objection of the greatest seeming strength; but on a serious consideration of it, its weakness will soon appear. We yeeld, without any advantage to our enemies cause, that what the Magistrat does as such, about Church maters and officers, he does it imperially and with dominion, and (as they use to speak) *Architectonice*: but what then? It proves the persons to be subordinat to the Magistrat in these his acts; but not the power in its exercise; nor the maters a-
bout

bout which it is exercised, for (1.) The Magistrat, when he by his irreligious and unjust carriage in his office, or otherwayes, becomes notoriously scandalous to the Church, is lyable to Ministerial admonitions, rebukes, seclusions from the Sacraments, &c. And is thereby subordinat to Church power, or the Ministers of Christ in exercing it about him; and yet the Magistratical power, and its exercise, is not subject to them, whatever resistence our opposits make to this mutual subordination of the persons of Magistrats and Ministers: yet they must either deny the Christian Magistrats the benefits of the Gospel & its ordinances, dispensed by Ministers; or els yeeld this truth. Is it not clear in other powers or relations? as suppone, one is both a Magistrat and a Son, is there not here a reciprocal subordination and superiority of persons with a coordination of powers, as is hinted above? We plead no more for the Ministers of the Gospel, and the Government of the Church commited to them. We grant a great difference in other respects, betwixt the Magistrat and Ministers; they act as meer servants, without all dominion in them; He with dominion and Magistratical authority over the persons of Ministers: yet for all this the powers are coordinat, and in their exercise not directly subject to one another. (2.) These powers, their exercise, and respective objects becoming reciprocally the object of one another (as the Ministry and its objects being one part of the Magistrats power, the Magistrat and the objects of his power, being likewise a part of the object about which Ministers exercise their power) under different formalities and specifications, there arises or results, not only a
sweet

sweet harmony, and a mutual subserviency to one another, in advancing of their respective ends; but likewise an indirect subordination to one another, in the exercise of their powers, without any dependance of these powers upon one another. But this subordination is only of the persons, and not of the powers: which by being the mutual objects of one anothers powers, does not subject the power, and its exercise, but only the persons; for any thing or power becoming the object of another, does not subordinat it to that power; the Word, Ordinances, &c. are not, by being the object either of the Ministerial or the Magistratical power, subordinated or subject thereto; so that the Ministerial power, its exercise, and the maters about which it converses, are not by being the object of the Magistrats power subordinated to it. This breaks the force of our adversaries Argument, which lyes mainly in this.

Obj. 6. It is only this sort of Supremacy and subordination, that the act of restitution does mean? *Ans.* It is not so, as is clear from the words and frame of the acts; for it is the Church assemblies, their proper maters, their constitution, the intrinsick obligation of their conclusions, that are subordinated to the Magistrat; so that all is nothing without him.

Obj. 7. All Divines, even the Presbyterians and independents in the Church of *England*, grant the Magistrat to be Supream in all causes, and over all persons Ecclesiastical; none of them scruple to take the oath of Supremacy, as it is established by law in that Kingdom? *Ans.* All Divines do not grant this, as is to be seen in the writings of many; and for any
thing

thing we know, it is not yeelded by the Presbyterian, and Independants, in the sense controverted among us; neither can it, seing it quyt overthrows, all Church Government, in its distinction from and independency on the civil Government of the Magistrat, which is contrare to the known principles, both of Presbyterians and Independants; and if the Prelats themselves durst speak their minde, conforme to their owne principles, they would not in this differ from us (as *Thorndike* more free and engenuous then the rest of his party does declame and cry out against the oath of Supremacy, as the great crying sin of the Church of *England*,) but to an excesse, would assert all, and much more, then we do, in this mater, were it not for fear of offending the Magistrat, on whom now they wholly depend, and whose Creaturs they only are; which hath in our times reconciled the *Prelatical* and *Erastian* principles, at least in appearance, that are most contrare to and distant from one another, yea more then theirs and ours. And although the Presbyterians and Independants, in the Church of *England*, do take the oath of Supremacy, yet it is with such explications, allowed & assented to by the Magistrat, that give it a sound sense, which was stumbled and scrupled at both in Queen *Elizabeth* and King *James* times, till its sense was explicat, and allowed; as is to be seen in the instructions given to justices of the peace, by Queen *Elizabeth*, for administrating the said oath; & Bishop *Ushers* explanation of it, approven by King *James*: In which sense it is understood & taken to this day among them. But to understand this mater aright, and to avoid the labyrinth of generalities & ambiguities, with which, some divines

perplex

tricat it; it would be confidered. 1.
a two fold proper supremacy, one civil,
Ecclesiastical, about Church power,
l maters. 2. There are two Kinds of
ose they call Ecclesiastical; some that
infically such, but in their nature, im-
nd use, civil, that, for their more remote
ects to things truely and properly sa-
d Ecclesiastical, as lawes made for the
concerns, outward liberty and peace,
rds and punishments, &c. Againe some
iastical are intrinsically and formally
shall preach the Gospel, & be invested
stery, or who shall be deposed from
l be rebuked, admonished and excom-
received and admitted into the Church,
e term e *CAUSES* is not here to be un-
physical, but moral and juridical sense;
uestions to be decided by those, who
d, either by God or men, to this work.
uestions, as they are the object of power
, are either proper and immediat; or els
remote. Hence we say 1. That the Ma-
ream Governour in all things or causes,
, relating to causes and persons Eccle-
judicial cognition and definitive judg-
belong to him, and not to the Church:
e admit the oath of Supremacy, & declar-
villing to take it, which was refused us.
Magistrat is not the supreme Governour
nd over persons formally Ecclesiastical;
t belongs to Christ Jesus only, and not
rat, as hath been proven above. This is
the

the supremacy, we deny to the Magiſtrat, and fo[r] which we have declined to take the oath anent it that is now eſtabliſhed law, being perſwaded (fo[r] the reaſons formerly given) that this is the ſupremac[y] granted by law; and underſtood in this oath. B[ut] 3. That cauſes and perſons formally Eccleſiaſtical are not the proper and immediat object of the Magi[-] ſtrats power, but only improper and remote, an[d] the reaſon is, becaus in the execution of Chriſts la[w] given to the Church, the judicial cognition and d[e]finitive judgment about theſe belongs not to the M[a]giſtrat, but to the Miniſters of the word; as for in[-]ſtance, it is not the Magiſtrats part to cognoſce an[d] determine, who is to be received into the Church and who not; this is proper to the Miniſters of th[e] Goſpel: and ſo of other cauſes and queſtions of th[e] like nature. *Obj.* Then the Magiſtrat, in protecting countenancing and furthering of the Churches ac[ts] and ſentences by the ſword, muſt be a blinde execut[-]er of them? *Anſ.* This muſt be ſaid out of envy an[d] malice; for (1.) the Church is the executer of h[er] own acts and ſentences, and not the Magiſtrat, wh[o] only puts to execution his owne lawes, that he [is] pleaſed to enact on her behalf. (2.) It is know[n] to all, that we grant to the Magiſtrat, (and to all i[n] the Church,) a diſcretive judgment to cognoſce o[f] the Churches acts and ſentences; and if he find them not to be juſt, he hath a definitive judgmen[t] anent the execution of his own Lawes made abou[t] them: for the obligation that ariſes from Church[e] acts and ſentences on all in the Church, to the obeyin[g] and furthering of them, is only conditional, and n[ot] abſolute; that is, none is bound to obey and advanc[e] the Churches sentences, except their mater be just and righteous, which must be first known before they finde themselves obliged to this. But here the immediat object of the Magistrats power and its exercise, about Church acts and sentences, is properly civil, and not Ecclesiastical, to wit, whether he will execute his owne law or not. These things are easy and plaine, and if ambition and worldly interests had not determined many to the contrare, there would be little controversie about them.

Obj: 8. The Magistrats power and its exercise about Church maters and meetings, being independant on the Church; what he does in relation to Church concerns, determinations and sentences, he may doe it antecedent to these, without the Church. *Ans.* We deny the consequence to be universally true: for some of the Magistrats sentences about Church maters and meetings doe necessarly suppone, the Churches sentences and acts, for their object; as these of ordination, excommunication: acts of regulation &c. must necessarly pass, before the Magistrat can reach the persons and things, to which they are applyed: for instance, before the Magistrat can doe justice to a Minister in his maintenance, he must first be ordained, & by it have right thereto, on the Churches act of ordination; which must first be known to the Magistrat, and by him given as the ground or reason of his sentence, for the Ministers legal right to enjoy and use the provided and allowed maintenance; and so of many others. We grant, in some cases and things, a power to the Magistrat about Church maters and meetings, which he may exercise, antecedent to the exercise of Church power;

M   he may

he may, yea, no doubt, he ought to command Ministers, when negligent, to their work or duty, without a Church sentence, yea contrare to it: but to say, that the exercise of his power, in many things and cases, is not necessarly subsequent to the acts and exercise of Church power, is most absurd, & abhorrent to all right reason; seing there are many things that the Magistrat ought to doe to and for the Church, that necessarly suppone, not only the being, but the exercise of Church power, without which the Magistrat cannot doe: how shall he punish contumacious, heretical and excommunicat persones till they be first dealt with by the Church, conforme to the rules of the word, and declared to be such, &c. The reason of the consequence is weak; for all created power suppones its object, and in its exercise must be subsequent and posteriour to it; which is not inconsistent with the independency of any power on another; as is to be seen in the instance of the marital power, and others; the power of the Magistrat about it presupponeth the conjugal relation, & its acts, before it can put the laws in execution, anent it, in application to the persones under that relation. The designe of this objection is obvious, which is, to evert all Church Government, the necessity and use of it: but before it have its full intended force, it must first be proven, that Church power and its acts are competent to the Magistrat, and may be done by him; as that he may ordaine, depose, receive into, and cast out of the Church, preach the word, dispense all ordinances, &c. which no *Erastian* hath yet done; for if these be incompetent to the Magistrat, and are to be done by others, the former conclusion will hold. Con-

Concluſ. Haveing thus, with all Chriſtian ingenuity and plainneſs in the words of truth & ſoberneſs, diſcovered our hearts anent the foregoeing particulars: we expect that much charity and juſtice from all, (even our Antagoniſts) that before they give out their cenſurs, they will ſeriouſly conſider, what is ſaid, and in the ballances of Scripture and true reaſon, impartially ponderat the reaſons and grounds of our judgment and practice: leaſt, in ſtead of fighting againſt us, they happily be found to fight againſt God; for ſeing the grounds, on which we build, are of common obligation on all Chriſtians, and on which, our Chriſtian profeſſion leans; none can refuſe our concluſions, but they muſt either contradict and ſhake the foundations of the ſaid profeſſion; or els ſhew their inconſequence, and inconſiſtancy with theſe: we have not inſiſted on, nor much made uſe of particular places of Scripture, nor wrangled (as many in their debaits doe) about the ſenſe and application of theſe, nor laid the ſtreſs of our arguments from antiquity on citations from particular fathers and hiſtorians; but on the ſeries and threed of theſe ancient records; to which we appeal, anent the maters debated in the preceeding diſcourſe: as any, that deals candidly and impartially, will, on trial, find. The iſſue of our adverſaries arguments, in the defence of the *Antitheſes*, reſolving in theſe three, the imperfection of the Scriptures; the manifeſt and violent perverting and wreſting of them; the profeſſed and open contradicting of their authority, by *Hobs Leviathan*, and others more groſs, (if groſſer can be) do ſufficiently declare, what the tendency of the contrare opinion is, and what we may expect,

expect, will be the result of the same, if things continue, for some time, in their present channel. All Protestants, before these debats entered on the field, esteemed the perfection of the Scriptures, the chief and principal foundation of the reformed protestant Religion; and builded thereon their doctrins, in opposition to popery: which, the patrones of prelacy doe now strick at, and labour to shake, in denying their sufficiency or perfection, in maters of obedience or practice; whereby they break the force of all the arguments, that the Protestants used against the Papists, for the fulness and perfection of the holy Scriptures: and the truth is, prelacy cannot be maintained without this assertion; as is to be seen in the most eminent assertors of it: for if we hold the Scriptures to be a perfect and full rule of faith and manners, and not to be receded from, in maters of doctrine, worship and Government; the prelacy controverted, having so little evidence from them, it cannot stand, and if this sufficient regulation of the Scripturs be refused, what a wide door is opened to humane inventions; and what may not men bring in at it, to the corrupting and polluting of all the Churches concerns? We grant, the admitting of the Scriptures, for a pairt of the Churches Canon and rule, seems to draw a barr on much of the Romish trash, (which is condemned thereby;) but does not the prelates boldness, in violenting and forceing of them, in answering of our arguments, and maintaining of their concepts, remove this barr, and lay the door open, for what they will? for howbeit the Scripture speaks, against the worshiping of Creatures, Images, Angels and Men, and chargeth these practises

ctises with idolatry: yet *Thorndike*, and most of the now prelatical gang, purge the popish masse, the worshiping of the host, of the virgine Mary, Images & Saints, from idolatry and superstition. How impudently bold are the *Erastians*, in wresting the Scriptures, used by their antagonists; in which they are not inferior to the *Socinians*, and the most noted hereticks of the Church; but we must say, with lesse shew of reason; as will be evident to any, that will compare them together in their comments. What security can the Church promise her self from these mens principles and wayes, who build their conclusions, on such foundations, which if once admitted overturns all? But alas! when to enlarge the Magistrats power, and to give support to their wild assertions about it, the divine authority and doctrins of the Holy Scriptures are boldly contradicted; and all Religion ultimatly resolved into the Magistrats Conscience and Lawes; as *Hobs Leviathan*, *Parker* & others, undertake to make out, against the foundations & superstructurs of our Religion, are they not thus pulled done to uphold the Magistrat, & to extend an immense power in him? but, we hope, to the external shame, confusion and ruine of the cause for which they contend. How much doe we finde that saying of *Pauls 2 Timoth 3. 13.* verified in these men, *evil men and seducers shall wax worse and worse, deceiving and being deceived?* but our confidence is, that *their folly being made manefest to all men, they shall proceed no further*: for the cause which they oppose is Gods, and that which he must owne and plead; seing the Royal prerogative of his absolute Soveraignity and Supremacy, are intrinched upon, and

M 3 struck

struck at, by his Creatures, the wormes of the earth; who, contrare to their indebted and profess'd subjection to him, assault his throan, and invade the regalities of his high and glorious Crowne, which he will uphold. OH that all, ingadged in this warr against the Lord and his anointed, would read and consider the *Second Psalme*, and yet hearken to what is there foretold anent the issue of it, which will be sad and heavy to them, that obstinatly set themselves in opposition to Christ and his Kingdome. Let none that side with Christ in this quarrel, be affrayed or ashamed, to appear in its defence against all sorts of opponents; for as we have the full light and evidence of the Word of God, to justify its righteousness, from the reproaches of men: So we have the righteous and Almighty God to take our part, who, on the account of his justice and Supream dominion, is ingadged to owne them, that owne him in this cause. In contending for these, we contend not for honours, dignities and the riches of this world; but only for the Lawes, Ordinances, and Servants of Christ Jesus, and that obedience and subjection to him in them, that he requires of all in his word; yea for the Royal dignities, & supereminent prerogatives of his righteous and glorious Crowne, which the Father hath placed on his head; giving him a name above all names, that, in the name of this JESUS, all knees should bow, yea shall bow. Who needs to be affrayed, who owne such a King, and have him on their side, who in his own persone overcame & Triumphed over all his enemies;& yet againe will doe so, in the persones of his weak, contemned and persecuted servants & people. The Lord build up the walls of Jerusalem, & make her a peacable habitation. Amen.

www.ingramcontent.com/pod-product-compliance
Lightning Source LLC
Chambersburg PA
CBHW020907230426
43666CB00008B/1345